Immigrant Songs

The poems, fiction and letters of Saro D'Agostino
Collected, edited and with an introduction

Immigrant Songs

The poems, fiction and letters of Saro D'Agostino

Collected, edited and with an introduction
by Antonino Mazza

QUATTRO BOOKS

The publication of *Immigrant Songs* has been generously supported by the Canada Council for the Arts and the Ontario Arts Council.

Cover design: Diane Mascherin
Cover image: Oil painting by Saro D'Agostino painted in mid-1990s.
Typography: Grey Wolf Typography

Library and Archives Canada Cataloguing in Publication

D'Agostino, Saro, 1948-2000
    Immigrant songs : the poems, fiction and letters
of Saro D'Agostino / collected, edited and with an introduction by
Antonino Mazza.

Also issued in electronic format.
ISBN 978-1-926802-90-9

    I. Mazza, Antonino II. Title.

PS8607.A28A17 2012   C811'.6   C2012-900337-9

Published by Quattro Books Inc.
89 Pinewood Avenue
Toronto, Ontario, M6C 2V2
www.quattrobooks.ca

Printed in Canada

. . . I, escaping to words
learned nothing:

still trying to say
I love you father
through a senseless English poem

Contents

Immigrant Songs

Poems in Order of Publication

Unpublished Poems

Letters

Appendix

Bibliography

Introduction

Immigrant Songs is a collection of the extant poems and fiction of Saro D'Agostino, together with a selection of his letters. Although at the time of his death in 2000 Saro had never published a book of his works, his friends related to him wholly as a poet and writer. He was a dreamer, a lover, a traveller, a mentor, who wrote some of the most remarkable poems to come out of the Italian Canadian literary experience of the 1970s, which flourished after the arrival of unprecedented numbers of immigrants following World War II, especially from the South.

Indicative of Saro's unmistakable literary talents is the ripple effect that the few poems of his to appear in the anthology *Roman Candles*[1] caused among attentive readers of contemporary literature. Scholars respected in their fields – Loriggio, Amprimoz, Boelhower, Pivato and Teti[2] – signalled the poems' merits even as they were giving fresh consideration to the impact "other" (minority) writing was having on an earlier, less generous definition of national literatures. To be sure, Saro himself, almost as a matter of purity, was never one to promote his work, even at the plentiful public readings in Toronto for which the city is celebrated. Nor did he take part in the scholarly gatherings that proliferated as literary studies became infused with multicultural perspectives.

Significant in this volume, perhaps, will be the discovery of an inner logic in Saro's writing, a seemingly natural development in content and form that is a telling element in important literature.

---

[1] *Roman Candles,* edited by Pier Giorgio Di Cicco (Toronto: Hounslow Press, 1978).
[2] See bibliographical notes for F. Loriggio, A. Amprimoz, W. Boelhower, J. Pivato and V. Teti in the Bibliography of Secondary Sources.

Saro's very first excursion into print was with a poem published in *Impulse* magazine[3] in 1974. The poem was based on Alex Colville's painting *Horse and Train*, which had achieved iconic status among a generation with its appearance on the cover of Bruce Cockburn's 1973 album *Night Vision*.

Alex Colville's Horse

Alex Colville's Horse
is plainly in for it.
He's already dried mince-meat
on both sides of the tracks.
But just over the horizon,
where the rails meet,
Van Morrison skirts along
like a folksong in his Lees,
and you can hear the rails
humming louder, "This is the
train, this is the train…"

It is thrilling now to imagine how the editors of *Impulse*, the cutting-edge magazine of contemporary Canadian writing, might have read the easygoing expression "… is plainly in for it." The casual language delivers a devastating and ironic *fait accompli*, dealt by an unknown poet with a remarkable feel for the English language. The poet's attention then passes through a rapid succession of images and turns back to a thing coming from over the horizon and beyond, back to the fixations of a generation that recognizes the rhythms of a Van Morrison blues in a train track. A

---

[3] The first eight issues of *Impulse* magazine (1971–1990) were edited by Peter Such, who, in his recent editorials, had defined contemporary Canadian writing as being as diverse and experimental as contemporary Canadian society. Lester Dennis was co-editor of this issue.

fortunate beginning, these lines – they are the young poet's first spike planted upon the literary landscape to which he sought entrance.

This was no lucky first strike, no fluke. An intuitive logic binds the contents, form and intention of Saro's work from beginning to end, linked to a desire for another world, for a new beginning. We can perceive the full potential of this gift of unity if we consider a work that appeared as a prose piece the same year in *Waves* magazine[4] and was later reworked as a poem. "Saint-Denys-Garneau, an Autobiography" may rest as one of Saro's most accomplished poems to have come down to us, one that we sense belongs to a larger canvas of Canadian letters that includes the poetry of Quebec. A grand poem of light and shadows, therefore, by a new Canadian voice, devoid of historical Anglo-Franco prejudices. A poignant "autobiography" of the founder of modern Quebec poetry against the backdrop of that province's recent history. The October Crisis of 1970 must have been on Saro's mind, as must have been the language question: language is a constant preoccupation with Saro, and a central theme in his prose as well.

But Saro had the true soul for poetry. His "autobiography" of Saint-Denys-Garneau focuses on the poetics that inspired him to see, on the streets he is walking, a *vision* of human tragedy with which he strongly identifies. Who will not be touched by the out-of-focus story of a shadowy foreign poet encountered on the streets of Toronto who, having published his collection *Regards et jeux dans l'espace* at his own expense, suddenly feeling his poems unworthy, runs back to remove all copies from the bookstores and burns them?

---

[4] The prose piece with a similar title, "Saint-Denys-Garneau: 30th Anniversary," was published in *Waves,* vol. 3, no. 1 (1974).

Though this prose piece is by far the lesser of the two works, I hope that its inclusion in this volume's Appendix, along with an earlier version of Saro's poem "Immigrant Songs" (1976), will help reveal the poet at work, revisiting and reworking his themes and language.

This is the collection of Garneau's poems that in later years would be recognized as revolutionary, the first modernist poetry of Quebec.

The drama does not end here. Saro's poem goes on to a description of the poet's desolate death, *imagined*, since no one was present to witness it, which skirts on the prophetic.

Saro's personal story is of course an immigrant story, the story of a foreigner in a new country. His story might appear indistinguishable from the stories of the many sons of recent immigration. However, Saro's life took a divergent trajectory from a tender age for the rare and original talents he developed, for the depth of understanding of his own condition, and for the difficult circumstances of his displacement. Increasingly, his life included a growing affliction with depression, which he took heart to defeat but which ultimately took such a tragic turn.

Rosario (Saro) D'Agostino was born on July 11, 1948, in San Nicola da Crissa, a village in Calabria. He was born to older parents. His mother, Rosa Deraclea, and his father, Nicola, married in 1929 and had their first two children early in the 1930s. Rosario was the second child so named to be born to Rosa after Nicola's return from the war years in East Africa and POW camps in Kenya and then Scotland. The first son born after Nicola's return had died at fourteen months, in May 1948, lacking medicine, of pneumonia. Rosario, at his mother's insistence, was named after his dead brother, who had borne the name of the religious confraternity that her family had supported for centuries.[5]

The abject poverty and misery following the war meant that millions of Italians sought opportunities for gainful employment elsewhere, no matter the difficulties. San Nicola da Crissa was one

---

[5] San Nicola da Crissa has two competing confraternities, one devoted to the Santissimo Crocifisso, the Most Holy Crucifix, and the other to the Santo Rosario, the Holy Rosary. The Deracleas had played an active part in Santo Rosario for centuries and, according to Salvatore D'Agostino, Saro's mother had wanted to devote a child to her confraternity for the safe return of her husband after so many years.

among hundreds of towns in the South that was losing most of its inhabitants to migration.[6]

By 1950, Nicola was working, already at an advanced age, along with hundreds of other Sannicolesi in Toronto.[7] His sacrifices paid off for him in postwar Canada's fastest growing city. By 1952 Nicola sponsored his eldest son, 21 years of age, who worked as a tailor. Rosario, still a young child, arrived in Toronto with his mother in 1953. A married daughter, Caterina, arrived the following year. With their rural attitude towards saving, the family soon was able to purchase their own home. Nicola thought he could now return to his own country. He acted on his plan in 1960.

When his father decided to sell everything and go back to Italy for good, Saro, nearing his teens, returned to his place of birth with his parents. His father recognized his mistake almost immediately and came back to start again in Canada, leaving Saro once more with his mother in San Nicola. It was not until 1962 that they were all back together in Toronto.

Saro spent the two intervening years in San Nicola da Crissa, in the ancestral house perched high at the upper end of Via Alpina. One imagines the children running down the steep dirt path in front of the house to the bottom of the hill. Most roads were still unpaved in the village. There was little for the child and his mother, changed by their seven years spent in Canada, to look

---

[6] In his two-volume history, *La Confraternità del SS Rosario in S. Nicola da Crissa* (Catanzaro: 1989 and 1996), Domenico Carnovale, Saro's tutor in 1961, reports the devastating demographics of San Nicola da Crissa: from a population of 5000 in 1950, the town registered only 1900 inhabitants in 1989 (vol. 1, p. 7).

[7] The story of the migration to Toronto of the people of San Nicola da Crissa is almost legendary. San Nicola anthropologist Vito Teti charts not only the departure of the people from his home town but also the departure of its very soul in his book *Il paese e l'ombra* ("the village and its shadow") (Cosenza: Periferia, 1989). He describes as well how Toronto's Sannicolesi found ways to replicate the village's ancient social and religious structures and re-establish the two confraternities.

forward to. The houses had no running water, there was no refrigeration, laundry was still done by soaking and beating clothes against a smooth rock by the edge of the torrent.

To enter middle school, Saro would have to take the entrance exam. He walked every afternoon, rain or shine, to the school principal's house to be tutored privately. Domenico Carnovale lived on Via Garcea, at the opposite end of town. Saro was a good student. Within a year he had covered the required review and passed the entrance exam with excellent grades. On the expectation that he and his mother would return to Canada, however, he never registered for middle school. Italian was his best subject, although the local dialect made it the most difficult part of the test even for local students. So it was quite an accomplishment for Rosario, remembers Domenico Carnovale.[8] His brother Salvatore, seventeen years Saro's senior, also remembers that on Saro's return to Toronto in 1962 he spoke Italian perfectly. *"His having gone back had been a good thing for him,"* Salvatore says.

Saro's later friends know little about his teenage years in Canada. In 1972 Saro graduated from York University's Glendon College with a degree in English Literature. Barry Olshen, who became Saro's lifelong friend, was one of Saro's professors at Glendon. They met in 1970.

Someone else who knew Saro well at that time is Sam Pupo.

---

[8] A number of anecdotes persist in San Nicola about Saro's return to the village that ought to be mentioned in light of the tension that reappears in his writing many years later. Tino D'Agostino, his cousin who was two years his senior, recalls a calm, lively teen who was very smart and always liked to join in the fun with the others. The village children thought Saro was really spoiled, though, Tino continues, as his mother could afford a fresh egg for him every morning. The other children were envious. One day, a handful of children on their way to steal cherries were surprised by a snake. Tino describes how the kids all turned to sticks and stones to kill it, and then cooked it. But Saro wouldn't taste it. Domenico Carnovale has his own recollections of the youth. He remarks how respectful Rosario was in his home, and even remembers how well behaved he was serving mass at the confraternity.

"I was friends with Saro's nephew, Mauro.[9] We were in high school and Saro was at university. He was about five years older than us. In our walks we'd go down to Page Street, near Christie and Bloor, where Saro lived with his parents. We'd throw a few pebbles at his window, and he'd come out, and then we walked to the Bloor Inn at Bloor and Bathurst, and stay all night, and he talked of literature and music, and we'd soak it in. He became like a brother, a mentor to us."[10]

Sam Pupo is now a high school teacher in Toronto. He knew Saro's parents. *"His father,"* he tells me, *"was a very quiet man. He was a soldier in the army and had been away for ten years, and when he came back he must have been shell shocked, or perhaps that was his personality, but it was very difficult to get any words out of him. Saro didn't know him very well. Whereas his mother was the exact opposite, she was a wealth of information, always chattery, chattery, chattery. She wanted to know, asking questions, making comments, always. And Saro was very close to his mother."*

How was Saro's relationship with his siblings? *"His brother and sister were much older. Saro was an enigma to them, I'm sure. He had integrated in a different reality of books, of a new culture. Sure, he had his foot in both worlds, but he was almost a different generation. Saro had moved on – and he had this story where he had been in Canada for a number of years and then went back to the village, and then had to move back here and relearn the language."[11]*

---

[9] Mauro is Saro's nephew, his sister's son. Both Mauro and Sam visited Saro in Greece. Later Mauro went to live in Turkey as a teacher and writer.

[10] Page Street is in one of the working-class neighbourhoods where many Italian immigrants lived and puchased their first home.

[11] In an interview, Saro's older brother Salvatore attributes the distance between them to lifestyle (marriage, house, mortgage) as much as to age: *"Io con Saro non eravamo proprio, forse perché io ero sposato, lui faceva una vita diversa della mia. Delle volte avevamo delle discussioni, e lui diceva, 'Ma io son contento così come mi trovo. Voi pensate che per essere felice debbo avere na moglie, na casa, nu mortgage....' Come se il suo mondo era un mondo diverso dal mio, non avevamo rancore ma vivevamo in due mondi diversi. Questa distanza c'è stata."*

In the poem "Wake," and especially in the poem "Immigrant Songs,"[12] Saro deals explicitly with the enormity of the silence that had imposed itself between the generations, between children and immigrant fathers, between the irreconcilable anthropologies that resulted from the displacements and dislocations, and the cultural transformations that occur with migration. But to do this with the apologia that will satisfy Saro, which is the full argument for a right to one's own life's choices, given the guilt children feel in stepping away from their parents' struggle – despite his father's seeming magnanimity: *"My father forgives me anything"* – Saro must move on not only spiritually, but must remove himself physically from Toronto as well.

In the summer of 1973, Saro travelled to Europe – Holland, Germany, France, Italy – and visited his village in Calabria that August, but only briefly. In Florence he ran into Glen McGuire, who had been another student of Barry Olshen at Glendon. The two became fast friends and arranged to meet in Samos, where Glen was meeting other travellers, among whom was another Torontonian, Susanna Stewart.

By the time Saro met up with Glen, Saro's Mediterranean sensibility had been captivated by the opportunity that Greece seemed to offer to find the freedom he was seeking. It became the country to which he would return numerous times between 1973 and 1979 for extended stays with friends and lovers, with the project to be *free from the harness of a settled life in Toronto* and to write.

Saro had two long and fulfilling love relationships in those years. The first was with Rita Davies, with whom Saro stayed in Samos several times between 1974 and 1977;[13] the next was his

---

[12] Saro published the poem "Immigrant Songs" in two versions. The earlier (1976) version is reprinted in the Appendix. The later version, presented in this volume with the rest of Saro's published poems, appeared in *Roman Candles* (1978) along with four other poems.

[13] Rita Davies studied English Literature at Glendon College and went on to do a Master's degree in Drama Studies at the University of Toronto. In later years she worked in the cultural office of Toronto City Hall.

relationship with Jocelyn Laurence, with whom he spent an extended period in Corfu.[14] Some years after the end of both these relationships he married Susanna Stewart, and their daughter Sarah was born. Saro obtained his Ontario teacher's certification and for several years taught grade school in Toronto. When this marriage ended in divorce and he was diagnosed as suffering from depression, he took an extended leave. Saro never returned to full-time employment, but sought to continue to write. Little was seen of his writing efforts thereafter. By now he was frequently under the influence of prescribed medication and substance abuse.

The years following 1983 are the time that Saro's friends refer to as the dark period in his life. There was a reprieve. In 1987, Saro was married a second time, to Lis Jakobsen. That same year, on the insistence of friends,[15] he contributed a superb surreal prose piece, "The Feast of St. Joseph," to *Gamut International,* which he described as an excerpt from a novel in progress.[16] It was among the last works he published.

In spite of Lis's care for Saro, things would not get better, however, as Saro was afflicted with severe depression. In a letter to Barry Olshen (Toronto, May 13, 1991), Saro lists treatments he had undergone and how he had reacted to some of them. In the same paragraph he alludes to electroshock treatment, which, despite its tarnished image, was in the mid-1980s once again "emerging as the treatment of choice for the most severe depression when drugs and other therapy fail[ed] to help."[17]

---

[14] Jocelyn Laurence is a Toronto writer and the daughter of Margaret Laurence, one of the major figures in Canadian literature. Saro wrote about Margaret Laurence's visit with Jocelyn in Greece in the summer of 1979, while Jocelyn was with Saro there (letter to Glen McGuire, Corfu, July 14, 1979).

[15] Alfredo Romano, Mario Romano, Haygo Demir and Antonino Mazza, all of us editors of *Gamut International.*

[16] Saro referred to each of the two fictional pieces reprinted in this collection as a novel in progress. Whether or not they were parts of the same intended novel we cannot say. I am treating them as two separate pieces of writing, since each stands well on its own.

[17] Daniel Goleman, "The Quiet Comeback of Electroshock Therapy," *New York Times,* August 2, 1990.

To be sure, no one can know with certainty what treatments Saro was undergoing at the time he wrote this letter or over the course of twenty years of therapy. Nevertheless, even if the treatments never included electroshock– as Barry Olshen and Saro's wife, Lis, are clearly convinced was the case[18] – they make up an impressive list of "iatrogenic opportunities," in Saro's words: a series of medical gaffes, or (to be charitable) disappointing failures, that Saro narrates with crisp irony. At the same time, Saro's letter reveals remarkable restraint and even modesty in the face of the scientific claims made by doctors and analysts. (He retracts some criticism of the profession he says he had made in quoting the novelist Italo Svevo.) Throughout the letter shine Saro's deep introspection and intellect. We read it with concern for the man and for the fragile support for his cognition and creative imagination.

In reading Saro's two fictional pieces, "The Feast of St. Joseph" and "Maria," therefore, we ought to keep an open mind regarding what a work of literature, what a work of art ultimately is, or can be, as it relates to human cognition. It is Northrop Frye who reminds us that "it is not a nation but an environment that makes an impact on poets, and poetry can deal only with the imaginative aspect of that environment."[19] Both these stories, the only two that we know to have survived, written in Toronto near Christie Pits park, not far from the working-class neighbourhood where Saro grew up, travel far towards subconscious worlds.

----

[18] Lis Jakobsen convincingly dispels the notion that Saro might have submitted to this treatment (also called electroconvulsive therapy, or ECT). Here is Lis's answer to my direct query on the subject: "Saro never had ECT. There were a number of occasions when this was a possibility, but nothing was ever carried through. Each time, Saro either talked himself out of it or he was talked out of it. Whatever people's recollections are, I can tell you for a fact that he never received ECT." Although some friends of Saro's think otherwise, Lis's statement here coincides perfectly with the recollections that Barry Olshen previously shared with me.

[19] Northrop Frye, *The Bush Garden: Essays on the Canadian Imagination* (Toronto: Anansi, 1971, 1995), p. 166.

The landscape, the environment, to use Frye's term, is dislocated to the extreme in these stories. A topographic map of Calabria – where Saro spent the two years that coincided with the end of childhood and the beginning of adolescence – thoroughly spectral in its detailed representation of the persistent Southern question, is spliced together tightly with notions of North American popular culture. In all of it (as some will notice), Saro's personal stories seep in.

In "The Feast of St. Joseph," wanting to alleviate his guilt of forty years, the drunken protagonist writes a letter to the priest who had heard his confession when he was a youth in the village. The man wants to come clean on a lie he had told the priest at confession, in retaliation for the priest's insinuation that when he was a child the man had caused the death of his baby brother in the womb, as a punishment from God for blaspheming. By morning, as the man progressively sobers up, the cascade of lies that had held the story together falters, and the man determines rather to mail the letter of his confession to a Hollywood studio.

If "The Feast of St. Joseph" leans towards surreal notions of referentiality, stylistically "Maria" represents a leap forward in Saro's fiction. The meandering in the much later "Maria" is more pastiche, storytelling as pure self-reflexivity and intertextuality. There is no way of knowing, of course, what the final results of Saro's efforts to write a novel might have been, had he more fully succeeded in his intentions as he expresses them in this passage from "Maria":

> *Tonight it's not the courage of underwater men I want to fathom, not the depths of God's regrets (his precious apologies became tedious long ago), but just to see if the ending of a story makes any sense of the beginning, just to see if at the end it turns out I was the stand-in or the passer-by or the hero or the villain of the tale, not to find justification or meaning, but just to know, like a child learning a new game, if the first tries really count. Not to drink for nothing, in other words, and dodder through what's left, regrets in hand, appraising the geometry of the stars and*

dispensing explanations for what happened, excuses for what didn't.

One thing is certain, however: there is no dead language in all the surrealism in his fiction. No matter how dark the darkness, or light the subject, there is sustaining humour, a desire to know more, an unmistakable irony that is all his, as we see in all his writing.

Ever analytical, alert, guilty, often fun, delicate, and well-informed, there is only literature of a higher order in all the work in this volume, not least in the selection of Saro's letters. These are letters that Saro addressed to some of his longtime friends and lovers, who kindly agreed to share this privileged window into a poet's soul. I am grateful for the mettle that each one of them has shown, as it could not have been an easy decision to divulge private letters and intimate material going back as far as forty years, in some cases, that can no longer be given their full context.

Our intent here is not to be curious onlookers. Rather, it is to visit with Saro, to know him as the mentor that he was at times, to get an inkling into his sense of place, his geography, his maps: The map of a young Italian Canadian immigrant getting a job where he translates for his people in a municipal office in 1970s Toronto – and sending out across the street for an espresso. A map of his deliberations on the subject of cats, which he put into verse. A map of his search for a song he has heard in Samos, a song that is about "love" of woman, "love" of nation, until unexpectedly in a taverna one night two women get up and dance to that same song, a dance that showed the world the song is about everything.

Finally, our intent is to know the map of the truer orientation of Saro's world, as he writes even in the midst of his blackest moments of analysis: *"This much, though, is simply true: there's still a part of me, a place in the soul or the heart, that belongs more to infinity."*

Saro's words map his passion, his life's thoughts on the creative act of poetry, fashioned in a language that was not his own at birth.

Antonino Mazza

Ottawa, February 2012

The choice to use the title of Saro's poem "Immigrant Songs" as the title for the whole volume was inspired by a note in which Saro asks for a letter of support, and in so doing describes the publishing project he has in mind: *"I'd like to put all my poems together in a volume that deals with immigrant trauma and reconciliation."* I hope this posthumous volume will succeed, in part, in doing for Saro what he envisioned.

IMMIGRANT SONGS

Poems in Order of Publication

Alex Colville's Horse

Alex Colville's Horse
is plainly in for it.
He's already dried mince-meat
on both sides of the tracks.
But just over the horizon,
where the rails meet,
Van Morrison skirts along
like a folksong in his Lees,
and you can hear the rails
humming louder, "This is the
train, this is the train…"

(1974)

Slow Death

Saviour, believe me I keep
from falling without any act
of timeless faith, without
going back to the mystery or
comfort of the rising and
setting sun. Instead,
I learned how to ring my hands
around my throat and make
the blood boil in my eyes.
And even though this too
is just a little bit heroic,
it's taught me steady rage
and the sureness of slow death.

(1974)

Someday

Someday, honey
we will go to France
and stroll
along the Seine
and dance
with French abandon
in Left Bank bars
the chicken Frug
and la Décadence

(1974)

I used to

I used to mistake her singing
for some peace, until I saw
her singing Love's Old Sweet Song
while calmly detaching the wings
from a butterfly that wandered in.
She looked up at me and she said
she was tired of singing and all
my poems about the fortunate fall.
Then she laid her hands palm-up
on the window ledge, dusted
off the powdery wings, and leaned
over to watch them float down,
and she turned again, and softly
said, no more songs, no more
peace offerings, no more
lullabies to an untiring world.

(1974)

Saint-Denys-Garneau, an Autobiography (*)

I must disguise this

allow that his life was forged
by a new Quebec, old students
dreaming other lives, old days

>Nelligan singing
>his poems to the Virgin
>Notre-Dame, midnight 1899

Both Quebecs are far away
and I'm finished with spreading rumours
that the FLQ will soon avenge your death

You will not be an omen

Your photograph will return
to a certain number of dots
grey and black, a rectangle
>merely out of focus

>Still, walking down a Toronto street
>cluttered, grey-black and winter
>I hear the flutter of coats, another
>chill in my pockets, a chunk
>of sky focuses into white and I catch

*A note on the author accompanies the publication of this poem in
*Applegarth's Folly: Saro D'Agostino emigrated with his family to Canada
from Italy in 1953, and is still unemployed.*

myself thinking it was you running
into bookstores, hurrying
to get your hands on any copies
of your Visions still around and
set fire to your games and
watch them burn again

Regards et Jeux dans l'espace, 1937

———————

I'll let your journal stand on its own,
scanty details of several impossible plans,
indulgent arguments with the blank paper
      in the desk drawer somewhere
      in the infinite reflections of your Manor,
      Sainte-Catherine de Fossambault, 1943

Here we'll see that the Jesuits never left you,
the old Church of your mother turned more real,
like the monsters your games grew into
      You argued out of control

You nailed an iron cross to your chest
and how you grew and swallowed it into your body
is no more to me than
      a tree trunk overgrowing a nail

———————

Imagine, before all this
you made me dream
of myself as a well,
an open circle
for sky and trees

34

I was deep and dark,
a water at the bottom
of a spool of light

And I would have leaves
fall firey to drift down
my wide eye,
to float on my black
ocean, touching me:
to know you were
really there

———————

I thought I knew your landscapes
and I would find the edgeless dance
in the motion of your brushes

pictures for our Lady
to heal our jagged hands

And I would have leaves

———————

Now I no longer want to know
how your dreams clotted in your nostrils,
how a passing thought, a piece of sky
sharpening into white...
and suddenly the crystals of snow
are hardened into steel

You drop your brush on the leaves

I must stop here, I've already said
too much to write a poem for you

I must stop here at the brush in the leaves
and not turn my head up
to see perfect sparkling
crystals cut into your arms

It is enough for us to stop at your beginning:
the dance, the game
the words of footsteps
filling your solitude

The overturned canoe
your head lying face down in the river
is merely bad poetry

——————

I'll stop before all this
and learn to delight again
in how you had invented the night
to illuminate an uncertain star

——————

And still your cousin survives
her endless reflections in the Manor,
enduring
because you tried to call light by its name
and she thought the light would answer

——————
——————
——————
——————
——————
——————

When I was 16 the FLQ organized itself
to take revenge on the country that killed him

> They too
> speaking white
> and dreaming other lives

Le Devoir appeased them with eulogies:
he had written the best religious poem
to appear in modern times, canonization
was in the air, Dominicans pointed out
the real hole in his heart, his pure
return to the precise God

> *Et je prierai ta grâce de me crucifier*
> *Et de clouer mes pieds à ta montagne sainte*
> *Pour qu'ils ne courent pas sur les routes fermées*

while the Jesuits spoke of courage
and Quebec gave him to Nelligan,
John F. Kennedy, Pope John XXIII

Even in Ontario, we do not want to know
exactly how he died, there are legends
but the French books all say the same thing:

> On October 24, 1943
> Saint-Denys-Garneau
> was feeling anxious

> He paddled his canoe
> to an island he once
> painted, he began

to gasp for air, he
staggered towards
a certain house for help
and his body
was found beside a stream

His cousin enshrines his bones in mirrors,
convinced that he offered himself to light
and that the light accepted

(1975)

Corfu Afternoon

There is a redness missing
from the air, something
that will never break out

The sea claps its hands
and brings entreaties
from far away red places

and still, the time-quieted
cadmiums, Venetian dreams,
hollow the streets –

you were never here

You come closest
on deserted squares
at sunset, the orange
of a forgetful sun, sprinkled

like old flower on the rows
of white sheets stretched
across the balconies –

a short truce
between my loneliness
and the emptying sky

(1977)

Gifts

There are still premonitions
of love and cruel fathers
hanging in the dresses
draping the streets
of tourist shops, and I still
find myself mouthing
bits of lonely folksongs
as the expectant faces
float by me, but when

I see the moon between
the edges of these eroded
houses and just then
feel the softness of your neck
across my mouth, I know

that it is all a question
of happy fathers walking
briskly home with parcels
underneath their arms

(1977)

Travel

It is small here

The lights of the next village
press closer every night

but even in the darkness
the world here is the space
from town to the far
end of the mountain

A small island
in endless time, I sit on the balcony
and watch the stars close in, already
drifting down behind the ridge

where the mountain
drops sharply into the sea

There, the city drifts
across entire continents in plain
hard space, and time is not endless

only a little ahead of the present

There, the street-cars roll
down St. Clair Avenue, along a string
of lights opening the whole sky
and they never draw closer

There is always a madman
sitting well towards the back of the car

I was always peeking through
the white corduroy curtains
over the live still wires, standing

in the window like a sad song
in the night, between a lonely madman

plotting with eternity and
a claustrophobic tourist
holding back the starlight

(1978)

Wake

The women are in one room, the men
in another. Zio Crescenzo died
three hours ago. The women line
the walls of the living room, the
only light comes from a candle
in front of his picture on top
of the television set.
The women wear only black,
only their hands
and faces are visible. Some
of them have been wearing black
for more than twenty years, Zio
Crescenzo was the second youngest
of seven children. My mother
is the youngest.

         I have been taught
death is the mother of beauty, but
my family takes death less seriously.

The men are sitting in rows of chairs
lining the walls of the kitchen.
The sons are crying with their heads
buried in their arms. My mother
and father and I kiss each one, their faces
are covered with tears.

In the living room the women have begun
to wail and scream as though possessed
by demons or death itself. Later on,
in the middle of the night, it will
become a chanting.

              Another brother dead,
and she still stays up all night
to cry the pain of his life, learning
nothing more than ageing from all
the others:

              Salvatore,
found in a ditch in Argentina
with a knife in his back, Stefano
killed with an ax over some Calabrian
point of honour, Tommasino
who made it big in America and died
a lonely American death, Saro
who was born in a bad year and died
simply because half the babies
of the village died that winter.

The women will cry until the chant
is broken and one of them collapses.
Then some of the men will enter
and try to help them, but the cries
and chants soon begin again.

                    In the
middle of the night cousins will drive
down from the suburbs with hot coffee
which they will serve in demi-tasses.

(1978)

Canadian Poet

That thin northern acrobat
now shows me feats
of poetry, 5BX plans
for leaving fine imprints
on this endless snow, as if
to ornament our mere survival

I tell him it's the ice
that's spread so far
and keen that human eyeballs
crack

He tells me my sunless face
and sunken chest
are bad examples, weak
impressions

I am sentimental, we
no longer speak to each other
To him, a palm
bleeding under the snow
would indicate poor health

a need for exercise, proper
diet

(1978)

I Ching in March

We wait for poems, scatter
coin tosses on sidewalks

we look for stalks
and cracked turtle shells
to appear at our feet

for any lapse
in the fixed pattern
of branch, for any
suddenness of air

We walk steadily, no wild
hexagrams grow here, only
the open conspiracies
of branch and time, melting
snow in even seasons

The signs are clear
but we still look aside

to water trickling under
the exact ice, escaping

on tangles of cement
cracks, live snares

that would set off poems
or more miraculously

make us lose our step

(1978)

Immigrant Songs

My father forgives me anything:

the senseless universities
that did not make things
any better after all

my vague Canadian pain, even
my Protestant friends
ashamed of their money

He has forgiven Canada
for his old age, he has forgotten
the war-crazy rich who took him
from his family, twelve years
in blasted foreign countries, wars
he did not understand

And still he goes to Mass
every day and still he prays
for those who ended up alone

while I, escaping to words
learned nothing:

still trying to say
I love you father
through a senseless English poem

I
In Toronto they remember
the Calabrian sky, a tourniquet
in their stories, swollen
summers, women in black

Death binds their endless
families, a chain
of arm bands from the blue
mangled South to College Street

Here there is no famine
their tall children
speak good English, here
the South bleeds quietly

II
Blood flakes congealing
on Canadian daughters
on their hidden lipstick
and dreams of fair
Canadian boys, congealing
over their aching, foreign
southern cunts, a twisted
seal of southern love

Blood flaking like clay
on the work boots of the father
walking home, another tourniquet

Sister, we are bound
your clotted blood
to our father's boots
he too dreams of the red
blood running, the family fire
Sister, look
at our loud weddings
the eyes of our fathers
bleed with joy and ache
with love, anticipating
that unbound moment
when the new husband unwinds

the first night sheets
in triumph

III
Sister, let us set
our mangled blood
on even louder fire
and burn all whose
souls and lands
do not run red

IV
This young man that I know
born in a village not far from mine
laughs about leaning back
from the desk in his chair
slowly, further and further
until he is about to fall over,
all this after having placed
his father's anvil strategically
behind him, so that he would break
his neck if he went too far
When he tires of this, he pins
his back against one end
of the room and dashes for
the opposite wall with his head
firmly forward, always stopping
as he puts it, within a hair's breadth
I told him that at his age
I merely wished my family
and all Calabria dead a few times
before reaching for the Valium
and putting Cohen on the stereo

V
Poetry at best
leaves me cold

my father suffered more
indignities than words
could ever dream
of conjuring

this is no way to avenge
his or any strangled life

He suspects I am unhappy
because I write, it resigns
him even more

that after all these
countries and all these
losses, even his youngest
son will not escape

I should leave poems
and this language and
I should blow up
all the sub-divisions
he carried cement for

He did not build my prison

I cannot raze all these
countries, Father
I am sorry for these songs

(1978)

Poem

There is no way to serve you

I will no longer offer you
the pain, feed your scorn

You have taught me
that after all, this is only
the world, we make gestures
we misunderstand, we should

feel grateful for the whiff
or two of good intentions
floating through our lives

I will no longer serve you
this embarrassment, from now on
I will remind you: it's either
that or politics

(1978)

Looking Back (*)

I remember your eyes when you loved me

and then it's not just another story
of the will turning itself inside out
to keep the heart from stopping

I remember your eyes before we lost touch
with what we saw, before the heart
turned to memory – a great jasmine bush
outside our window, the moon splashing
across the sea and folding itself
in the pillow, ready to spring
when you moved your head – sometimes

it was the sea we made love with –
sometimes we forgot, and it was the memory
of the sea that we undressed and mounted

(1978)

*Saro included a photocopy of the published version of this poem along with a
handwritten note to Rita Davies that ends with the words: "The poem comes
from our recent times."

Seduction Poem 2
(Love and Death)

When your hair was as careless
as the branches and shone
like silver birches
there was talk about the leaves
of your fingers, silent music
and how a touch
could change the world

The truth is your hair
doesn't even shine like the moon
all your boyfriends lied, it shines
only like clean hair

It doesn't sound the mysterious
chords, at most I'd give it a simple
counterpoint of pain, and that too is a lie

I am not even angry
that it can do remarkably well without me

The truth is you've lynched a couple
of us there, and I would like
to live a little longer still

(1981)

Unpublished Poems

I have another spy dream   (*)

I am on the run again

this time with the microfilm
of the plans that would save the world
Forces from all sides
are closing in to kill me
and have the world
as it has always been

In the morning you wake me
with eyes full of love and comforting

And I turn away from you
like a double agent
who cannot remember
what side he woke on

(1976)

*Unpublished poem found at the start of a long handwritten letter to Rita Davies.

Scruff at Ephesus (*)

He walked slowly across the circle of the stage
where thousands of years ago men long dead
were young and yelled their lines in rage

He snuffed along the crevices still cracked in African woe
and smelt things with no meaning
here where nothing grows

And turning his head up at the sun meowed
if kings and men would only know
that a palace of stone for the loud and the proud

can't replace the fish on the dish.
Old Scruff, common sense cat, turned and went.

(1977)

*Unpublished poem found in a typed letter to Rita Davies that bears the title of
Saro's projected book, *The Whiskered Image: An Anthology of Cat Letters.*

Breaking the Ice   (*)

We do not recognize ourselves
There is no time
We are always jumping

We are no more than familiar faces
long time acquaintances
we never really got to know

There is no time, we are too busy
building lives to jump from
It is only just when we are ready
that we may wonder
where and how it was we met

We have never met, we were always
leaving – there are songs
that make us cry, there is the way
a man waits on the streetcar island
with his lunchbox at midnight
and it's freezing, there are
fields of flowers that are glad
to see us go, there are telephone
calls from former wives – there are
a thousand reasons for leaving
when the only sense is poetry

We cry our hearts out and the sun
comes up to scratch the ice
It teases us to stay and start again
We begin again, a crystal of hope
here, a grain of forgiveness
there, haven't I seen you somewhere
before, another field of flowers,

a crack on the ice for a ladder,
another scaffold to build, one more
renovation of the face, don't
I know you from somewhere –
We were falling from our dreams
into the busy oblivion of daylight

(1977)

*Unpublished typed poem found among Saro's letters to Rita Davies, written at Saro's apartment on St. Clair Avenue in Toronto.

LETTERS

To Barry Olshen

Samos, Greece [1973]

Dear Barry,

It was good to hear from you. Athens was being punished by 118 degree heat for the defacing of the city with political propaganda, but your letter took me out of the weather for a while. I've been on the Island of Samos for about 2 or 3 weeks, just off the Turkish coast, birthplace of Aesop, Epicurus, and Pythagoras – a trinity that in its wholeness must mean something. I'd like to be able to stay here for a few years – there are hardly any tourists, and even though I don't speak a word of Greek, most people treat me as one of the family – perhaps because of the Italian / Greek saying "stessa faccia, stessa razza" – "same face, same race". The referendum abolishing the monarchy is over, proving only that the time is ripe for 100 well-armed Byrons. But the States, I think, needs more than Byrons – it should claim an error in the 1776 Revolution and give itself back to England and our gracious queen. <u>Even</u> in Greece, coming back from <u>Turkey</u>, people aren't given the same kind of treatment you received at the border. The <u>International Herald Tribune</u> is having loads of fun with the Watergate developments, – while much of the European press seems to be too amazed to say much. Fascism seems to be blossoming all over though – <u>all</u> political organizations without parliamentary representation are banned in France; Italy is about to take the same measure with the excuse of the many recent right-wing bombings. If there's going to be universal messiness, I'd prefer the Italian high-spirited confusion, where general strikes are called at the drop of a hat and where chaos is a spirited way of life. I realized in Florence that a lot of me is peculiarly Italian – I felt at home arguing and waving my arms, but that cold northern seriousness has probably penetrated too deeply into me and I still look for reasons to bemoan mine and the human condition. The thought of leaving the life of Samos and coming back to Toronto to prostitute myself in looking for a job doesn't thrill my Mediterranean soul – most jobs make it difficult to remain a sweetly drunken monk and writer of sea-poems. Perhaps a more secluded "saner" place, like the Glendon ambience could help keep the peace. In the meantime, I've been re-reading <u>The Magus</u>. I met a Glen McGuire in Florence, and we soon realized that we both knew you – he was the fellow – I think – who talked to you of some connections between the Tarot and <u>The Magus</u>. It also turned out that this white-hatted fellow and I were both intimate with Sharon Mason. He and a Swiss girl and I and my New York Jewish girl have been travelling together for over a month. He is writing quite a bit in Samos, while I am losing more and more of language – they say that when this demon of language departs, it takes the angels with it – but the sea, and clean Greek light are keeping the good angels lazy, too content for any flights. This contentedness (and lack of money) is also keeping me from going to Israel – I think I'll stay there for a long while on my next travels.

I still think a lot of you being a father, of your baby, and it makes me feel good. It's good to think about the beginning of a really fine family, of a man who's going to make a great father and a woman who'll be a lovely mother. Perhaps it's my Italian background that makes this occasion mean so much to me – I'm really happy for it, and I wish all three of you the greatest health and happiness. I hope that Toni's really well, or that whatever discomfort there may be is forgotten in happy expectation. I look forward to seeing both of you soon. I love you both.

Be very well,

love, Russ

Toronto, May 18 [1978]

Dear Barry,

I'm sorry I haven't written to you in so long. Every once in a while I start to think that I have written to you recently and I begin to wonder what I said. There's been so much shit and garbage falling out of an excuse for a sky and seeping through the pavement that I'm afraid of having sent you sad, scatological letters. Then I realize I've been maintaining my famous reserve and I have not written to you at all. I've attempted high, spirited letters, but it didn't work. I want to say white and blue and beautiful things to you. I'd like to be able to show you how much better off the world is to have you. Instead, I think of you. I've been thinking about you a lot, imagining you brushing gainst blue and white under a real sky in a real land, getting your beard tangled with God's.

Your letters are magnificent. They bring joy and a sense of passion. And then I start to worry about you coming back to Toronto and its Weekend Star version of life. I imagine that if we keep on our toes we can have a Saturday Globe & Mail edition of life here, but that's no warm heart pastry either. I think it may be hard for you to re-adjust to this huge shopping complex of a city. Nothing has changed, except for more stores and more shopping centres. I'm looking forward to your company more than ever, but I'm still a little worried about the passionless city that you'll be coming back to. Unfortunately, I've adjusted all too well here. Last week I noticed that the trees had leaves on them, and I don't know how they suddenly got there. Suddenly, it's hot and humid but it still feels like winter.

Please excuse the typescript. I'm at work and I'm probably looking busy, although there's nobody here to look busy for. I am a Clerk III at a Site Office of City Hall. My function is that of a Public Information Officer in Italian and English, but nobody seems to need any information, so I have nothing to do except for the occasional translation into Italian of municipal garbage. Luckily, I'm on my own here and I can have cappuccino and espresso brought from the bakery across the street in real cups and saucers. And I have an electric typewriter to type my poems. I wear white pants and fetching little Italian shirts out of defiance. I get paid accordingly, but it doesn't matter because I don't have to worry about moving into a better apartment or buying a car. There are definite advantages to not earning much money. Every two weeks I visit my superiors at City Hall and I flirt with the Language Clerks, who are all beautiful. I then arrange for a car and chauffeur to take me back to my office. I've discovered that even a lowly clerk III can be treated like a VIP if he is not intimidated by his lowly status. I was lucky to get the job (they say), not because I don't have to do much, but because many were called and only I was chosen. The only reservation the hiring committee had about me was the state of my health. I assured them that even though I look thin and closer to the next world than to this one I am in virile aggressive health. But because of the poetic nature of recent events, my statement was open to doubt. I had to call up the first day and say I couldn't start work because I was sick. I was sick at heart because Rita and I weren't getting along at all, my poems were being rejected, and the shit had been accumulating for a long time. I assured them I would start the next day. But that night was given to the demon rum — I couldn't sleep and thought a few drinks would help. By three in the morning I was solidly drunk. By five in the morning I was sick. By seven I was still drunk, and like a drunk I put on my suit and tie and went to City Hall, rehearsing an appropriate excuse for 45 minutes on the streetcar and subway. I arrived at the perfect line: "I'm sorry to have to do this again, Mrs. Kelly, but there's been a death in the family and I really have to go now. I will call you tomorrow." I asked the security guard for direction to Mrs. Kelly's office. He stepped back and looked at me as if I were a terrorist. I mumbled and walked away. I finally found Mrs. Kelly's office and as soon as she appeared I blurted out "I'm sorry

again, there's been a family in the death and I have to go now."
She said, "Won't you please take off your coat?" Like a fool I did
and some lowly bureaucrat appeared out of nowhere, took my
coat, and disappeared into nowhere. Mrs. Kelly then told me how
impressed she was with my qualifications and began a lengthy
explanation of how city hall worked, an explanation to which
comments on my part were not necessary. I interrupted her with
a mournful "I really have to go now." I was dying. But she took
me to meet someone else down a long corridor. I thought she
was taking me to the hospital. This other woman asked me to sit
down and immediately began a lengthy explanation of the
computer system, of the yellow cards and the white cards. I was
just about to say, Yes, but my face is green, when I noticed my
coat hanging on a rack. I jumped up, grabbed my coat, and ran
down the long corridor. I thought I would explain to Mrs. Kelly
as I ran by her office that I because I was a poet everything was
alright. Instead I tripped over a little swinging door and found
myself on the city hall floor. When I came back the next day,
sober, it was as if nothing had happened.

These kind of events haven't been too unusual lately. Since
coming back here everything has been a little strange. Our friend
Kordas had to borrow the money to go back to Greece [. . .]

Both Rita and I have job offers from Nicos's school in Corfu,
starting in September at $3500 a year each. That's not much
here, but it's enough to live on in Greece. There's a lot of reasons
why we shouldn't accept the offer, besides the obvious one of not
knowing whether we'll still be together or not. If we (or I) take
the job it means that we wouldn't be able to save any money to
fix our house in Samos. It also means a two-year commitment
and leaving a bunch of debts behind in Canada. Still, isn't it
better for my biographers to say he spent two years teaching in
Corfu rather than he spent two years as a lowly civil servant in
Toronto. Our minds will be made up soon I hope.

I'm afraid I may have given you the wrong impression of things here. It was really bad for a while, but despite the shit I'm beginning to affirm and be who I am. I don't allow the town planners to talk to me too much about town planning. I bring up Plato with them and express my concern over the mythos over logos argument. I bereave the death of stoicism with "community organizers", talk about the supernatural powers of Catholic priests to people who talk to me about their analysts, I go to Malcolm Muggeridge lectures, I tell planners that they don't really understand Ivan Illych because if they did they would quit their jobs, and I am charming in cafes and jazz nightclubs. I am also becoming less dogmatic and more sympathetic.

[written in longhand]

In short, I am becoming more Italian. I even hang around with Italian poets whose women are leaving them and we shake our heads lyrically over the lack of passion in these times.

May 26

[continued on the same page in longhand and with the same pen]

Rita is leaving the day after tomorrow. She's terribly in love with me, terribly attracted to another man, and quietly half-asleep. I know there's not another one like me in the world, so it's too bad for her. Anyways, as word of our "break-up" gets around, girls begin to call me and offer to take me to Greece, editors begin to accept my poems, I get invited to do readings, and Rita is much nicer to me. I'm beginning to accept the situation gracefully, and I know enough that her rejection of me is her mistake. I'm not taking it personally. I guess what I'm trying to say is that I'm interested in the Superior Man, quality, and the good. I've been very fortunate to have had a lot of those things with Rita, but I accept the fact of change. My passion and my vision are not diminished. I'm concerned about her and the directions she's taking (this other man is, of course, a twerp), but it's a little tricky to help someone without pressuring them, especially in a situation like this. This calls for the old favourites, time and distance, and for another magic ingredient, gentleness.

I may be moving soon. If I'm lucky I may be able to take a friend's apartment on Roxborough Ave. It's very fitting – an attic apartment in a non-ethnic neighbourhood. I think it's not far from your place. I'm looking forward to seeing you, and the things you've seen. Toronto's not as bad as I make it out to be, as long as you know you'll always be leaving it. It's nice to sit in outdoor cafés in the evenings or go have a few drinks and listen to some jazz. There's also a lot of really fine people around. Passion still lives around little tables and amazing journeys in the night.

A whole lot of pages here, all about me. Even so, there's the memory of you and love for you behind these pages. Thank you for all the bits and bites and hugs, and for setting the world straight.

All my best, Saro

P.S. If you have time to write again, please write

> c/o Dovercourt Park Site Office
> 485 Dovercourt Rd
> Toronto etc.

Toronto 27 July 1984

Dear Barry,

Thank you for the birthday greetings – they were good to come home to. I started missing you as soon as I got back to Toronto. You're a good friend, which seems to be an exceptionally rare thing these days. I guess the same things that are making marriage and love so difficult are also making friendships difficult. But it always seems easier when you're around. There always seems to be at least a little something to celebrate in your company.

As you know, it's been a hard year with me. The hand I was dealt didn't leave much room for the imagination, and a lot of times it seemed I could only bluff or fold. Fortunately, folding is against my nature – I'm digressing – what I wanted to say is that your friendship and your company did a lot to help me see a little past my hand, to the happiness that can come from strength and faith (I confess, I do have a little of it) and the tranquillity that can come from knowing you're not deceiving yourself.

Sarah's marginalia (*)

It's good to hear that you're unambiguously happy in Victoria, free to leave things anywhere you want, just spending time brothering yourself. I get the same refreshing sense sometimes, like last night when I was in the kitchen, stoned and reading a friend's poems, realizing I didn't have to wash the dishes if I didn't want to, that I could listen to jazz as loudly as I wanted to at four in the morning and that I could go climb Scarborough Bluffs the next day.

---

*Saro wrote this next to an arrow pointing to his daughter's drawing on the body of the letter.

I forget that by the time this letter reaches you, you may have to put the cap back on the toothpaste again.

I spoke with you on the phone today, and after I felt like just getting in the car and driving west. Unfortunately, my middle-age reason stepped in and told me it would be a week's driving each way, even though I have some of Mario Andretti's blood in mine. Are there any Jewish racing car drivers? The cheaper airfares require advance billing and the train turns out to be quite expensive. I think that going west with you was something I should have done from the beginning. My trip to Florida with Giorgio was good, but especially for a poet he has less of a sense of adventure than I do. He was afraid of going 115 m.p.h. on the freeway and he didn't want to take the Blue Ride Skyway for a thousand miles because the thousands of dips and turns affected his bursitis. So we took it for only part of the way. Still, a magnificent road along the edge of the Appalachians. I enjoyed the holiday, the sun and the beach, but travel always makes me want to travel more. I wish I could come out to B.C. to see you, but the lack of funds doesn't allow it. In fact I may have to move or sell my car to get by on the 30% salary cut, or, as you suggested, get moving on making some money with my ideas.

I hope you're still unambiguously enjoying that lovelier part of the country, even if it means coming back with a bigger itch to go.

Give a kiss to Sylvia for me – and tell her I'm looking forward to more evenings like the last one on the back porch. And tell her I think she's wonderful.

Hugs and kisses to the gang of children, and a manly punch in the shoulder and tweak of the beard to you.

> With much love,
> Saro

March 21, 1991

Dear Barinsnakov, (*)

I made this set for you over quite a long period of time, mostly those moments, or hours, in the middle of the day or the middle of the night, when the writing had to stop and the music came on. The writing, by the way, pleases me much more that it ever has, even though I know I will never be the kind of person who knows if it's genius or drivel or journeyman work. But, the music: it's an alphabetical arrangement in four volumes of "folk" music of the late sixties. I think it's about a hundred songs all together, many of which you I'm sure you know very well and most of which I think you'll really enjoy. Some ranges, like the L to N or C-D, seem to be better than others, but I was surprised in the end that an arbitrary, alphabetical arrangement worked out so well.

I've been looking forward to giving it to you for some time, but since our shining paths haven't crossed as usual, I decided to write this note and drop it in the mail.

I hope you're as well and as handsome and as enthusiastic as when I saw you five days ago, and that you can take enough time away from le Français to figure out this fine, old Italian toast: ACQUA FRESCA, CAZZO DURO, proclaimed by all around the table with a serious clinking of glasses. In its original form, the lingua franca of Mediterranean sailors, relics dealers, and professional snake handlers, it may have been a hermetic palindrome and the closest you could get to being angry with God without being Jewish.

*A pet name that plays on the name of the Soviet ballet dancer Mikhail Baryshnikov, who had defected to Canada in 1974. The opening refers to a set of tape recordings.

But that's just an aside. Mostly I just wanted to say that you're a cherished friend.

Saro

[Pen drawing of Bob Dylan with handwritten note: *Bob Dylan in a Punk-Sadducee frame of mind, c. 1965 C.E.*]

May 13, 1991

Dear Barry,

I promised to respond concisely to the concerns in your letter. I tried to be as honest and concise as I could, but I think I may have left out (subconsciously on purpose, I guess) [my thoughts] about my own feelings and experiences with various psychotherapies. I neglected to acknowledge what you probably already know, namely that by this point in my life (almost 43, the age at which "traditional" analysts give up on any chance of success) the issue has become so loaded that I shouldn't discuss it with anyone, least of all with a very good friend who is interested in pursuing the discipline.

I'm not implying that I want the last word on the subject. This is just a correction, a postscript to the letter I mailed to you yesterday. What I'm saying is I don't think my quotation from Italo Svevo fooled you – by this morning it didn't even fool me. What may be closer to the truth is your suggestion that my own experience hasn't been particularly successful. After 22 years (off and on) and the expert aid and intervention of at least 20 highly trained specialists (of varying persuasions and fame) I don't feel any better off than before my million dollars or so of therapy. I understand the argument that I might now be <u>worse</u> off without the help of all these experts and their assistants, but being more or less rationally minded I also have to concede the possibilities that I could have been the same or better without their involvement.

And I don't mean to imply that I live purely within logical realms. In fact, I continue to see my psychiatrist every two weeks; and perhaps cutting down from daily treatment does represent real improvement. But I really haven't come to terms with all the iatrogenic opportunities in my therapies; what it means, for example, to have my treatment instantly terminated after many months of daily sessions because I had revealed one of my moral failures on the couch, to have another year of therapy abruptly terminated because I expressed the feeling that more electro-shock treatments would probably not help me, to terminate another analysis myself because the analyst insisted on remaining silent even after I broke into tears and pleaded with him to say something, to be informed by one of this country's more noted authors and practitioners that based on the fact that I was hesitant to place the Kleenex I had used to dry my tears into the ashtray (one could still smoke during therapy in those days) I was crippled (that was still a usable word in those days) by authority figures and that that was a result of my father's two year absence when I was a child. When I replied that as a smoker of many years I automatically did not place scraps of paper into ashtrays, he said that that was one of my defences. According to others I was variously eating the wrong foods, punishing myself, protecting myself, Oedipally unresolved, psychotic (for which I was prescribed a phenothiazine – still the "drug of choice" in mental wards and hospitals – whose side effects (I discovered on my own) include tardive dyskinesia, lupus, and, in 15% of all cases, what is quaintly called "Parkinson-like disorders", characteristically described as "a fixed, emotionless facial expression (mask-like in appearance), a prominent trembling of the hands, arms or legs and stiffness of the extremities that limits movement and produces a rigid posture and gait"). When I complained to my therapist as to why I wasn't told there was a one in 6 ½ chance (a good place bet at the races) of ending up like that for the rest of my life she replied that it was still the best available treatment for psychosis.

I realize the irony that I'm indulging in a bit of therapy right now in this letter to you. And I remember that I promised to be concise in trying to be more honest about my Svevo remark. Perhaps I could have said only that I believe a lot of therapists have a lot of blood on their hands (none of it mine, perhaps), but it doesn't follow that you would be having any part in it. You were right to be angry and hurt that night. I was mixing up my personal and rational approaches again and behaving badly for the sake of – I don't know the why. I guess I could choose from the litany of "whys" in this letter. I think I can discount the psychotic and the wrong foods. As for the rest, I'm not sure. In my case, I'll try harder to remember not to behave the way I did with you that night. Nobody deserves that kind of treatment, least of all you, who has done no less than love me for a good many years.

Saro

To Rita Davies

March 12 [1974]

Taki's Café [Samos]

Rita,

How am I ever going to tell you what you do to me. I wish it were 1825 so I could shamelessly go on for pages and pages how none but the immortal poets could ever sing your graces, how no one but Botticelli could paint your hues – I would really like that. I really mean these things – I have no shame. I am ridiculously in love with you, even beyond the limits of good aesthetic sense.

I feel like I've been a little suspended lately, that I haven't shown you much of this, maybe because of the house-search hassles, maybe because the change in our surroundings hasn't quite caught up with me yet. But I haven't forgotten your graces and your hues. I keep on being amazed at how lucky I am to have your love – it fills all of me, and I hope that some day it will show even in my skin.

I hope it won't be long before my communicative powers (and my mind) come back to me – there's lots of things I want to say.

I thank God and you for the beautiful things you are.

All my love,

Stumbling Saro

[Samos, 1974]

My Dear Serranda Tessera (44) (*)

You're asleep, and I thought you might forget – anyways, please wake me up.

Ever Yours

Young Cat

P.S. Thank you for Kotsikas, and one of the most beautiful days ever. (**)

*Saro's transcription of the Greek for *forty-four,* a nickname he sometimes used for Rita.
**Kotsikas is the name of a cape in eastern Samos.

Toronto, apartment on St. Clair Avenue, 1975 (*)

God, I'm remembering a lot tonight, sitting in this chair. How every night in Samos I would thank God for all his beautiful things and another bright day. I'm remembering how I felt thanking him every night ────────────

I also remember thanking him here too, though not nearly as often, and I remember when I first started thanking him this way: Shortly after we started living together. O.K?

I REMEMBER!

Spain
The Blue Sea
The feeling of you
down on me
The rain the first
[. . . . .]

[written vertically, along the side of the page:]

I was going to write more, and then I said, The hell with it, I'm going to wake her up.

And finally I said, Well look at Mauro – he can be a pool shark and he can write a play. And he said, well what do you do when you have a father whose happiest moment was when his youngest

---

*Three pages, the first containing passages written diagonally, horizontally, and down the right margin, with a poem cut off at the bottom margin and Saro's drawing of a snorkelling mask; the second written in one horizontal paragraph; and the third containing two horizontal paragraphs and one passage written down the bottom margin.

son was admitted to law school. And I should have said, Then you put your fist through the glass. But I mumbled about saying Yes to it all, saying Yes despite it all, even putting your hand through a pane or two. And we drank and sucked lots of cigarettes and talked about all the gloriously crazy people, and we forgot for a while that his woman doesn't let him smoke because she loves him. And then he washed his hands and face with soap, and I gave him some Certs and we both hoped she wouldn't smell the smoke and get as turned off as he feared. And I told him that sometimes we're forced to be deceitful so we don't cause unnecessary pain. Minjin, I didn't believe it – AND I'M JUST WRITING THIS TO SAY HOW HAPPY I AM THAT I DON'T HAVE TO LIE TO YOU, AND THAT IF THERE'S ANYTHING HIDDEN it's probably hidden to both of us. And Oh God how I hate those times when I'm less to me and less to you. Though weak as I am I don't tell you often enough how bright you've made me. Minjin, you've made me very bright.

I feel guilty writing this. I should have told him not to wash his hands or take any Certs. And though I feel guilty, I did write it, and you should see it. It's getting a little strange now – just want to say I think of you this time of night – and that I hope we never lie.

[written vertically, along the bottom margin:]

Last night I dreamed I was an aging and slightly eccentric old English gentleman who was alone and wanted to have as many children as pegs on the ivory neck of a guitar he held in his hands. This old man found himself young (in his dream I think) and with two lovely lovers which he never got to make love with because he wanted to be alone with just one (either one I think) and that couldn't happen.

[Toronto, apartment on St. Clair Avenue, late 1975 or early 1976]

Rita, if you wake up before me ———

It's just happened again, that clear feeling of how much I like this home of ours. I was going to say apartment, but I realized that what made the feeling so clear was the fact that you're sleeping down the hall from here. Some of it is the clouds moving by so fast between the bright orange curtains, and the peach of dawn behind them. I must sound like a sentimental poetaster. All I really mean to say is that it's a fine morning and that I like the both of you.

[Toronto, apartment on St. Clair Avenue, 1976]

When we are talking I might look off into space because I never
before tried to tell you that you are more than just my happiness,
much more, — you're in my sadness too

[Toronto, apartment on St. Clair Avenue, 1976]

Dear Rita,

I am going to take you to Paris and momentarily forgive the French. I will give you six nights free accommodation and a tour. We'll go [to] the café where I read your letter three summers ago and experienced one of the most beautiful feelings that I've ever had. You know that my memory is almost non-existent, but I remember that café very well, even though I was there only once. (Sometimes I feel something that may be aligned to hubris – being so happy with you now, and going to beautiful places together, and being free – can we be aiming for too much?) Probably not – I've learned something very important with you in the last while: I don't have to "escape" anymore, I'm very happy (an inadequate word) with you already – I'm no longer looking for ease, – I just want to experience more of the world with you.

See you soon.

All my love,

Psaro

[Toronto, apartment on St. Clair Avenue, late winter, 1976]

Rita,

Before you go to your last Tuesday of work for a long, long time
to come, I want you to know that you are one of the most
beautiful ladies in the world, that it's you that makes me
beautiful. I'm already half-dithered, but if this goes on, if I don't
stand a little firmer when I see you so warmly asleep I may spend
the rest of my life as an illuminated sweet potato.

Thank you for all this.

Lorenzo Di Patata Dolce

[Samos, summer 1976]

I have another spy dream

I am on the run again

this time with the microfilm
of the plans that would save the world
Forces from all sides
are closing in to kill me
and have the world
as it has always been

In the morning you wake me
with eyes full of love and comforting

And I turn away from you
like a double agent
who cannot remember
what side he woke on

I can see it in the kindness with which you wake me in the morning. You must imagine there are thickets of lonely secrets and silent tortures in these nights when you're asleep and I'm just something a little more or less than lonely. Because to get me coffee you pass through this room I keep weighed down with years of cigarette smoke, bits of paper, and other hints of how tiresome these legends have become.

I wake up and see the coffee cup. I prop myself up with another pillow. I see the kindness in your eyes. And I take the cup and I turn away. I face the green shutter. You lie beside me, quietly, knowing it takes a long time for my senses to come back. My senses begin to come back as the green shutter comes into focus and I realize I do not know what to do from that minute on, what to do with the kind beautiful woman lying beside me. What to do with the green shutter. This day. I have had another spy dream and now in this peace and love and sunlight I have nothing to conceal and nothing to evade. I can think: dreams are tactics of evasion, by pointing to the truth behind your eyes they take away the realness of the day. And this too would be deception, another veil to hide the simple fact that I am not a good craftsman with love and light. When I turn away in the morning it is not for the side of truth. I am not a spy in God's service. The badge of truth that I like to wear was won in a long ago war, not even that, just an early minor skirmish with some cadets of ignorance. I do not fight any real wars. My dreams are just dreams. They distract me from my uselessness.

This is self-indulgent, and evasive. Just a prelude to a confession that sometimes I am not worthy of your love. I am misleading you with the long smoky nights. That table covered with coffee cups and bits of paper is neither a real nor a metaphoric rack. Basically these nights are spent evading time. By a hundred pointless tinkerings that give time the slip. I look a[t] pictures, I calculate how much it would cost to have a house, I write a letter to tickle the surface of my soul, I wash the dishes, I listen to a record I've heard a thousand times and time crumbles away completely, I talk to the cats, I write poems that start[,] I make better spaghetti sauce than poems, and get no further. I am not the man of my dreams, so if I seem the man of yours I think I am misleading you. Perhaps that is why I turn away in the morning. Like everybody else, my heart in youth seemed too large to accept anything less than the light of grace and beauty. I have seen some of it because of you. And I feel that I have failed it. I would say I'm being unnecessarily hard on myself if it weren't for the light you've shown me and for what you are.

You are more than any dream, and you are real. Most of what I do know to do with the day I learned from you. It's as if I were the After in a Before and After picture. I shouldn't go on this way. It seems that there is only the me side of it, like you are a mirror that makes me more beautiful. But I have also seen you. I have seen you more beautiful than anything I have ever seen before. I have seen you in days that could be nothing less and nothing more than <u>your</u> days. Maybe it is only this: I want the days to be simply mine.

I don't think I know what I meant here. I guess it's easier to put my arms around you while the city is screaming at the window and let our bodies warm each other with dreams of islands where the sun shines and we would stand out as beautiful as we really are, the beauty of our dreams. Any voguish paperback would say we never learnt to deal with Actuality. And I admit that I don't know whether I am just offering apologies for this particular weakness by writing this letter, or whether there are other truths that crowd the eyesight. But even after I look at the things I occasionally write down, and even if they strike me as at least analogous to something really going on, I wonder if once again I am not just being lured away by the dream of words and leaving actuality behind once more. I think about the dream of you and realize that you of everything in my world come closest to being dream and actuality, imagination and reality, meshed so well that either word becomes meaningless, and I can only say "beauty", or "your days are yours." The times when I drift away or I'm hardly there are the times when one word stands out above the other, the times when your weave of dream and real gets frayed by a hundred pointless little things that any other man wouldn't even blink at if he noticed. My disappearance when you're annoyed with the workmen or when I think the story you're telling is too mundane would probably have a neat term in some mediumvoguish paperback: amplified ego overcompensating for childhood rejections. Perhaps it's the same thing, but my soul says you are the marriage of dream and flesh and the day is not mine when this union falters, and I begin to disappear. I am afraid to say all this, perhaps for the same reason that I've written very little about you: words are dreams and you are more than dream. It's as if I would be giving you an imaginative reality that would split the day in two. You know my fear of words being their own truth. Maybe this has stopped [me] from "saying" as much as I would like to say. One thing I would like to say is please accept and love these things in me. You do love these things in me.

[...]

The actuality of an endless afternoon tangles up my insides and I begin to wonder what the hell I'm doing here. The actuality of the stars from the balcony, the cool night air like Shalimar, makes me feel I can find my peace and be in God's diplomatic corps here. Because there are these kinds of extremes in me, the dreams are important. Something that doesn't depend on the weather.

I don't know if I said much in this letter. As always, I get sidetracked. I wanted to write about you. I guess you're in all these other things too. Because you're with me it's no longer a question of getting out of the dark, but a question of making the best of the light we've given each other. I want to always be the most wonderful man in the world for you. When I am not I know that I am failing all our gifts and wasting the light. It's not easy being the two most beautiful people in the world, but that's the point where there is no difference between the dream and the actuality, where weather holds just a little power, and where – I do know this – our hearts really lie. So let's not worry about how easily we both lose perspective and go scurrying into all the corners. Let's be as friulindini as we are. As long as we remember where our hearts are, nothing's going to dent us for too long.

Always, Saro

Corfu, October 6 [1976]

Rita,

It all comes down to the fact that I am no good at all without you. I mean, I walk around and stuff and look at the trees and marvel over how nicely the Venetian buildings deteriorate, but there's something missing. Technically speaking it's like having a Ferrari Polpettini that doesn't have a distributor cap – it's very beautiful but it just won't go. In non-technical language, there's a certain redness missing, a redness that makes things just a little more than real, a redness that comes from you and makes it possible to feel the world around me. I've been trying to write a poem about that – because it is very strange – but even trying to write a poem is less red without you. I guess you're the one who does sleep in purple-striped nightgowns in the Wallace Stevens poem. That's the way I miss you most, though thinking about you so much of the time I realize that I miss almost everything. If anything, in these two or three days I've been re-assured that it really doesn't matter where we are as long as we're together, and that it's even more extraordinary, even more beautiful to know that we'll be in many places with each other. It was a grave sin for me to forget the redness as often as I did – I know I won't forget as easily anymore. If I could just hug you now, or feel your skin, or breathe in your red hair and fly calmly away with the birds outside our green window. [. . .]

Yours always,

Saro

[1977]

My sweetheart Rita,

I wish I could say it in a different way, because it's been almost four years and I want you to know it's stronger than ever – I'm crazy about you – you're a fantastic, very high, beautiful human being, and sometimes my mouth just drops open in the middle of the night. I'm sitting in the kitchen thinking about you, and I feel blessed. I do this often, and this time I want you to know it when you turn on the radio to find out the weather and I'm in my deep morning sleep. Please forgive me for the times when my stubborn ego gets in the way – it shields your light and makes me smaller. That part of me that's grown hand in hand with loneliness seems to insist on its misery at times and refuses to see the light. I'm sorry for this, because someone as beautiful and as giving as you deserves to have more of the light, your light, reflected back. I know I do reflect it back a lot of times, mixed with my own glow, but I hope that even in the shakiest moments we'll still have our lights dancing together, even if it sometimes means slow sad dances. But what a joy to know that we've still got a whole lot of lively jigs to do, sunny waltzes, hot jazz, and moondance.

With all that's good in me,

Saro

[Toronto, apartment on St. Clair Avenue, early 1977]

Rita,

Don't worry. After all, I am the walking one and only, my looks don't really abort cats, and we're going to Greece for a long time in just a few months. Most of all, I still love you even in fretful times. Think about all these things and you may find there isn't as much to worry about.

> Forever,
>
> Captain Cappuccino

[Samos, May-June 1977]

From The Whiskered Image: An Anthology of Cat Letters

Dear Rita Brown, (*)

It's getting to the point where it's either me or the cats. I don't quite know why, but that's where it's getting to. What I mean is, take tonight for example. There I was sitting on my guitar case on the floor of the middle room where we keep our snorkels and empty wine bottles, sitting there just watching Espresso eating the salami I had cut up for him. I had seen him hunting bugs in earnest so I figured he was hungry but too proud to ask. Anyways, in walks Mousha and sneaks behind the fins. I was afraid that she was going to pee there, but she's getting older and I was trying to give her more credit. Sure enough she started to pee on the plastic bag. I picked her up by the scruff of the neck, but do you think she stopped peeing? No. My life is in tangles, it's as if I were a ball of yarn that the cats like to scramble into a knotted mess on the floor. I thought I would come to Greece and write my book of cat poems. Instead, I have to hunt ticks on the kitchen floor and carry a cup of olive oil to drown them in wherever I go, I have to try to pick fleas from their fur (which the cats barely tolerate me doing even in their best moods), I have to get up early and go to town to meet the fishing boats and dish out a hundred drachs in fish a week and then Mousha won't eat and I stay up night worrying that she's going to die because that's the way it is here with cats; I have to go through moral dilemmas over whether to punish Mousha, should I hit her for shitting in the dining room where we have our 400 year old Turkish table?

*"Rita Brown" refers to the colour of Rita's eyes. Mousha and Espresso were kittens that Saro and Rita got from a farmer couple who lived across the road from their house in Samos.

do I just go along with the baseness of Pavlovian stimulus-and-response and teach her only through the threat of pain? is that the way the world really is? a Skinnerian jungle? would they really kill us and torture us if we were smaller than they are? Why do I like them so much? Is it because they represent innocence and spontaneity? because they are beautiful and agile and funny and deeply mysterious far beyond the Pavlovian muck? It must be all these things, but I only have two arms. Still, when we were on that archeological tour of Turkey with Earl and Mabel we did have the courage to admit that the most interesting thing we saw was the frogs and turtles in the ancient healing pool at Pergamum. I mean bits of old walls are bits of old walls, hardly worth zipping around in a bus full of retired dentists for two weeks. But life, that's something else. I don't mean to get too philosophical, Rita Brown, but it seems to me that we should be more concerned with the living than with the dead. Ephesus can't move, it just sits there like a heap of rocks, but Espresso darts his head and his eyes light up like Christmas trees when a leaf rustles in the wind. Well, I guess I've given away the gist of the first poem in my book – it's called "Scruff at Ephesus" and with all modesty I can say it's a good poem, perhaps a little too metaphysical in places, but you know what living in the clear light of Greece does to you. What the heck, I may as well let you read it now:

Scruff at Ephesus

He walked slowly across the circle of the stage
where thousands of years ago men long dead
were young and yelled their lines in rage

He snuffed along the crevices still cracked in Atrian woe
and smelt things with no meaning
here where nothing grows

And turning his head up at the sun meowed
if kings and men would only know
that a palace of stone for the loud and the proud

can't replace the fish on the dish.
Old Scruff, common sense cat, turned and went.

Of course all the poems won't be as "heavy" as this one, because
cats are more for lightness and gaiety; even when they're just
lying in the shade looking too grumpy to chase the spiders,
they're dreaming mythic good times, bravery, in orange sunsets.

I have to go now and make sure that cats can get down from the
tree – they like to pretend they're braver than they really are.

yours in love of <u>life</u>,

Herbert Stalk

[Toronto, apartment on St. Clair Avenue, November 1977]

Rita,

I realize I wasn't able to say what I really felt. It has something to do with knowing how much you gave me, knowing that it's enough to get me over the pain of your absence. I still think of myself as very fortunate. I was trying to tell you that that's the most important thing. I feel that more strongly than the irony and the regret. I hope you do too. We were too amazing to not think the best of each other now. I also wanted to say that your happiness is still very important to me. Although it didn't look like it during the high drama over lunch, I do have a better sense of things now, a better sense of myself, more faith in me, and in you. Someone once said (alright it was Kierkegaard) that the only people who never go back are gypsies and thieves. I guess it's even more impossible for thin gypsy thieves. It is too late, but that doesn't hurt as much when I remember that life is more important than wisdom and that I'll never lose the gifts you've given me. If you remember the times that I've shone, know that you had a lot to do with it, and if you see it again know that it's still true. It's here in between the words somewhere. At the risk of sounding giddy, I love the whole thing, and I cherish you for it. All my love.

To Pier Giorgio Di Cicco (*)

Giorgio

I'm applying for a
C. C. Grant (Explorations)   (**)
for <u>poetry</u> (of all things) –
They want to know how
"innovative", "creative" and
"feasible" the project is.
Only tell them I'm a latent
"Franciscan" I'd be happy
if you could write the
letter of appraisal
without mentioning junkies,
naked women, or Perry Como.
"Structural cowboy" and
"semiotic aphrodisiac" would
be much better –
Seriously (!) I'd like to
put all my poems together
in a volume that deals with
immigrant trauma and
reconciliation, and I'd be
very happy if you wrote a

*This note to Pier Giorgio Di Cicco was written in capitals on a narrow slip of paper that forces the text into an adroit verse format.
**C.C. is The Canada Council for the Arts.

letter for me.
Much love
and god bless you.
Il tuo, Saro

(1978)

To Glen McGuire

February 12 [1979]

Dear Glen, dear Glen, Glen!

Here's the latest facts:

1. We're listening to Bruce Springsteen, and every word is true. If you don't live in New York, it's still true. The backstreets and New Jersey and Johnny and Jungle land are still parallels, anagrams, metaphors, and icons of various places we all know so well.
2. All decisions should be based on songs.
3. We are deliciously crazy. We are beautiful losers. We are the world's wonders and hold an important spot in God's newsreel. (Imagine yourself in God's newsreel, what he plays before the Big Unknown future… "Today when McGuire [pan across the room to G.Mc. puffing on his Player's lights, hand still on his espresso, writing on a student paper] thought 'Estonia … the sea's the same everywhere … what is it about the blue … of airmail paper … had, I would give everything … how many roads … this room is the room that is all rooms … we sat besides many seas …'" and it all gets flashed onto the screen, returns like a slow cloudy fade-out to G.Mc. looking up at the pictures over his desk and fades into the coffee cup that gradually becomes the sea – there are continents approaching.) We're not even losers, just beautiful.
4. I probably will never stop drinking. Ouzo, especially, is very fine. It bridges a lot of distances, and for one that exists all over the place, that's very important.

5. All decisions should be based on songs.

6. I'm smoking Santé (unfiltered) and God, I actually like them! That's what's different about this time in Greece. I actually like the cigarettes. I doubt that anyone other than you could understand what that means.

7. You are one of the best songs.

8. The longer I don't see you, the more I think of you. It's getting out of hand.

9. I will never be the same again. And I doubt that I ever was.

10. The food and drink are always good. Except for the quick hamburgers we have alone. Even the little dry brittle sandwiches we have in Italian railway stations are good. Though the lunch packs they have are better – like you, I remember places by what we ate.

11. Eating together is like making music together.

12. All decisions should be based on songs.

13. The aesthetic / moral dilemma can be solved by eating together in a beautiful place while being outrageous and gentle.

God bless us all.

Saro

Corfu, February 22, 1979

Dear Glen,

I've resorted to the typewriter because I don't have any decent
pens. Even the ones I steal from my kids aren't any good. And
because I'm alone in the house and the clickety-click sounds
good, especially against the drone of the million frogs mating
outside, and the Greek music inside, of course I'm playing that
Greek song that followed me everywhere after leaving Samos last
time, the one I call "my tears are like Niagara". I finally bought it
a few days ago, after much mystery. Whenever I asked a Greek
what the song was about they would look up into the sky, utterly
unable to speak. If I pressed them they would say it had
something to do with love. If I then asked if it was the love for a
woman, they'd very hesitatingly say, yes… for the love of their
country? Again… yes… for the spirit?… Yes, again. Is the singer
happy or sad? Both. Is it about God or a woman? Both. I spent
half a class with an advanced group trying to find out what it was
about. They just looked at the ceiling and groped. I went to the
record shop and asked them for this famous Theodorakis song.
The man asked me to sing it. I hummed a few bars and his
friend smiled, left and came back with the tape. Then one
freezing night in a taverna in the middle of nowhere, the old
toothless Greek lifted the lid of the ancient Wurlitzer, yanked
out a 45 and plopped the needle down. It was the song. Two
ladies got up and danced, a dance that showed the world the
song was about everything. It was the coldest night I had ever
experienced in Greece, but even though I was half-frozen, it felt
completely right. The ladies were dancing, the old man poked
around the fire and explained how to make potency pills out of
the ashes, his wife laughed, and we all ate and drank too much.

I'm telling you all this because I'm suffering a dilemma I've
suffered at least a couple of times before. The facts are the facts:
here I am in Greece again. I have the opportunity of staying.

Nico is willing to hire both J. and I next year (which would solve the financial end of the problem). This life makes the utmost sense to me. It always has. As you know it can be very difficult and gripping to the core. And this time around has been more difficult than before: more isolation, less money, an exhausting job, a longer winter. Still, it's Greece. I just saw Equus a couple of hours ago. It reminded me of a very curious thing. Like the doctor, I could spend my life longing for what I already have. I mean, I could go back to Canada, work hard for ten years and become a doctor. Then I would have a picture of a Greek village hanging in my office and the village would be further away from me then than being a doctor is now. I guess I'm saying we're lucky, we already have a passion, we are already possessed by a daemon. But like you say, if we take poetry (or horses) seriously then we're in for a lot of trouble. As you see, I too have my doubts about law school. My main trouble so far is that I haven't been proved wrong about my meanderings – the world really is beautiful. If anything, I'm a more convinced version of what I was ten years ago. Nothing has dropped out of sight or transformed itself into something more "meaningful". I want to be a lawyer and argue for Italian construction workers from impossible Calabrian villages; I want to always screw the government; I want to be an English teacher on Greek islands; I want to return to Italy and show them that 20 years in Toronto has only fortified the pasta; I want to move to Victoria and spend my time infuriating and understanding you; I want you to photograph the possible and the impossible simultaneously; I want to write a history that's the real history and that people will not want to escape even though it's even more terrifying than the present versions.

Your decision to stop fiddling with the extraneous and just make pictures made me very happy. I always believed that photography is the right vehicle for you. Not a vehicle to anyplace (you're already there), just a way, not going anywhere on the usual maps, just something that you and the world do together. It would be good for both of you. I say that because of my keen critical eye and because I am happy that you taught me how to look. I remember fondly … the times you'd lend me your Nikon in Samos and say just enough, often not more than a few words, to make me see a little sharper. The fact that it's something I never thanked you for doesn't reflect my ingratitude as much as how good you were at teaching me – I didn't even notice it. It's quite a gift you have especially when I think of the lugubrious, dramatic and pedantic ways that I often go about sharing something. But what I meant to say was that perhaps you can get that quality into your pictures, perhaps they can sharpen or change the way things are seen in a way as simple and complete as you showed me five years ago in Samos. You're my father too. Just stay away from that Avedon-Hamilton shit. It's just as formal as deformed peppers, half cabbages, and translucent seashells. It's just decoration, which is fine on the cover of Vogue, or in the plaster and chrome living rooms of people who think they have enough money to understand nature. Don't get me wrong – it is, but only in name, Art. It's art and beauty with upper-case first letters. The lower-case stuff isn't so well lit.

I'm not championing the Available Light school and all their pyrotechnics, I'm just noting that you're a lower-case man – confess! Even in kindergarten you loved the small letters more that the capital ones! Too many photographers (viz: Hamilton) are screaming "LOOK AT ME. I AM ART. THIS IS THE WORLD YOU WILL NEVER SEE WITHOUT MY TALENTS." I cannot imagine you, pantheist, seeing that way. I think you're more apt to say, "This is a picture of a river god, looks just like a river, doesn't it?" I'm also glad about the 5X7 – river gods have a lot of detail. I must confess though that I'm not quite sure about the value of going to Sheridan. I know it's a great school, but if you could provide your own motivation it probably wouldn't be necessary. I confess. There are selfish motives here. I would rather you come to Corfu and made pictures here.

I realize now I didn't quite tell you what my dilemma is, at least its present incarnation, though I've probably mentioned it before. If I have, forgive me, as always. As I was saying here I am in Greece again, because I like the flowers and the people and this brand of joy and sorrow over that of Proctor & Gamble —— I just remembered, I have told you. Glen, what do you think? Should we stay here and continue old-fashioned obstinacy? Do you (think) we'll ever say No; I think that's over now. Italians are apt to say Non è colpa mia, è colpa dello Stato (It's not my fault, it's the State's). It works both ways. Is it my fault that the almond trees bloom in February? That the Greeks have such amazing faces? That my cat is beautiful? That this place makes J. and I cry and laugh, scares us to death and fills us with life?

Glen, there's so many things to talk about. I want to talk about your last two letters. They got into my bones. I want to talk about you and what you're doing for the world. I think it requires a pen, and a little more thought than what I am capable of now. Also, we have just run out of ouzo. When the owl hoots tomorrow night… for now I just want to thank you for teaching me how to see, in many ways.

With a lot of love,

Saro

P.S. – We got the tape, and it's magnificent. I think we're even starting to get into Elvis Costello. Once again, I wish I could do or say more than thank you.

Corfu, March 29, 1979

These are the most urgent of many points:

1. Are you definitely starting Sheridan College this September? Will you be living in Oakville? Wouldn't it be possible to quite easily commute the 30 miles or so from Toronto?

2. I will show uncharacteristic mercy as you glow over translucent shells and mutant peppers. I promise. I even understand. But I may as well ask this question right now: why do you want to be the master of the studio, the competent *dei competenti* with lights and arcs and other trickiness? Do you want to be mainly a studio photographer? Or do you just want to know everything? I can sympathize somewhat with the second reason than with the first. Even though I don't recall at the moment anything of much good coming out of a studio. This is not intended as a premature criticism. I'm willing to have my memory refreshed. In fact I just want to know if you are more interested in studio work than "field" work. And please understand that it's nothing more than these 9,000 miles between us that make me ask such dumb questions. I wouldn't have to ask if we were having coffee together. I'd know.

Despite the distance I'm still thrilled that you're going to be doing this. I still think it's the best road for you – in fact, I think it's almost tailor made for your perspectives and concerns. What better thing for a polytheist to do than to take pictures of the gods in everything.

3. The dream refuses to die. I have another five months here but I'm already plotting another return, another attempt to get something straightened out with the world. Even in my old age it still seems to me that the real choice is between disappearing up the asshole of suburbia (in all its physical and mental forms)

and disappearing between stamps in the passport. Neither alternative quite works, though I would choose the latter in a pinch. What's needed is a third way. What's needed is a new kind of <u>social</u> existence. I accept my limitations. I am not a genius or a pervert. The only thing I can really contribute to the world is an attempt to live differently, and to do so with other people. It is not enough (for either of us) that J. and I are here in an addressless part of a Greek island, living off god's spiritual gifts as much as off the few thousand dollars we earn. It's almost enough, but it isn't. It's enough if I didn't think of anything except myself. Then I can do my hand wash, take the reward from the children's eyes, celebrate the Spring, draw my little pictures and rejoice that we are eating meat tonight. That and a thousand other wonders of the Greek spring and a humanities background. But this Lake Isle of Innisfree is a little selfish. I need to share it all with others, people the island with a new kind of settler, not the one who has to clear the forest so that he can stand alone in his Presbyterian mantle, but the one who learns to live with the forest and make do with smaller yields if necessary. The one whose contingency plan is the sky. Yes, this is the old miserable Samos dream, not even in disguise. But, honestly, I can't think of anything else. It doesn't matter to me whether it's the Queen Charlotte Islands or the Dodecanese. As long as it's beautiful and god's face hasn't been pushed in, it's enough. What matters is that there's people like you and Jocelyn, and Mauro and Ra, and me, and everybody else whose vision isn't funneled by the crappiness that passes for modern life. Maybe I've spent too long in Greece but I'm appalled (really!) by the crappiness, jerk, empty goo-goo that magazines like Maclean's present as modern life.

Considering all this, coming back to Toronto in September might seem a little masochistic. I wonder if it really is. On the other hand, Corfu isn't the place to start these dreams, for reasons I can't really explain, and the present situation isn't really amenable to it. We've had the misfortune of not meeting any people who are anything more than adequately kind, polite, and very modern. They are nice people on the whole, but they seem to have all too well straightened out what's "real" and what isn't. Unfortunately it's been done exclusively along English survival-of-the-fittest lines. It's a nice little world where Catholics are weird, meaning is metaphorical, animals (especially dogs and horses) are important, and nobody-can-ever-know-my-deepest-fears. As a result I've gotten a lot quieter and retreated more into my personal Greek spring and bittersweet affairs with wildflowers and stars.

This is a long-winded way of saying I'm happy but I want more. I want to live in many houses. I want to try again, hopefully with a little money that we'll try to save in Toronto, hopefully with a child next time. I've put it all quite badly, but I'm still anxious to have your feelings on the matter. Write and tell me – One more thing I appreciate about you. You always do tell me.

With much love,
Saro

P.S. This is not another normal bugging you to come to the Aegean with us. P.S. There are a thousand reasons for doing it and only a couple for not doing it. It would be Sky-fucking.

P.P.S. – I've got another parcel, which I think is the book you sent me. I'll try to pick it up in the morning at the post office.

Corfu, July 14 [1979]

Dear Glen,

I just heard via Allison that your eyes are O.K. I heard about what happened via Eric yesterday and I was trying to figure out ways of calling your mother or someone who knew what was going on, but I don't even have an address where I can reach you.

I'm really glad it's not so bad as it sounded yesterday. The state of mind I'm in at times I almost feel responsible for it. I'm like a Graham Greene character that way – the nasty things of life are somewhat connected to my graceless state. That plus the fact that I still feel like a shit over what happened while you were here, that is, what didn't happen while you were here. I think the L's family became the Laurence Mafia in my eyes, and somewhere between crying bitter tears for David and his father's handshake, coping with what became painful parody of a self-obsessed writer after the fifth Scotch, feeling like I wasn't being treated any better than a gardener, collapsing with J., a year of constipated Brits ———— I lost myself in all this shit. I took it a bit too seriously because I'm weird that way sometimes, and I lost myself and the infinitely more profound connection to you. I hope I've learned something from all this – sometimes I think the only thing I really learned is how far gone I am. I mean, it shouldn't take much for someone to be able to meet family and friends at the same time, it shouldn't take much not to come across as a crucifix-waving gardener boy to one side and as a self-obsessed guilt-ridden Calvinist to you. The heart got lost somewhere, and I'm still looking for it. Greek summer always seems to bring on the wars – it's too bad that this time I can't keep the sides straight.

As you know, I haven't been having a good time of it, at least since Greek summer arrived. For reasons that I still haven't figured out the ideals which I spent so long in objectifying, tempering, clarifying – the simple heart, let's get excited, laugh for just being alive – got fucked up somewhere. Maybe it's because I've really started to see what I've been fearing for a while: retreat on all sides, dreams growing dimmer and more pedestrian, a questioning of the strength we used to take for granted, the big "so what" that comes after realizing that yes, I can make it, I can do anything I want to, but that I isn't the point at all.

Glen, please excuse all this indulgence – it's guilt, perhaps even the fear that this time around you won't forgive and forget as easily. In my last letter to you I said I didn't want to get into excuses for myself. In this letter it's exactly what I've done. The better part of me says all this isn't necessary, that it's my fevered paranoia still lingering on. If it is, I hope you'll forgive that too.

And in the end I'm audacious enough to know that my heart and my mind churns out so much stuff that some of it is bound to be good, if only because of the probability involved in sheer volume. I'm even audacious enough to still believe that those who understand, understand, that I haven't yet met someone who I wanted to understand and who didn't. I hope the gods don't strike me down for this but I don't really think there's anything wrong with being able to shine in only certain kinds of light.

I'm giving myself away again: how important it is to shine, how messed up I get when I don't shine. We gotta make 'em smile, we gotta make 'em feel good – I know no better ethic. Fuck Luther and Augustine and anybody else who never noticed their next door neighbour. Fuck the imperialists of art and anybody else who doesn't have the imagination to see that the world's in tears because people haven't found a suitable greeting yet. If our scientists and our geniuses turned their attention to that for a while.................. Fuck everybody who doesn't realize the good that's been smuggled across impossible borders from us. Darwin and Freud and Galileo and perhaps even B. F. Skinner are all absolutely correct, but that doesn't explain why I'm sitting here in a hot, hot night somewhere in Corfu with a bat flying around in the house, feeling like shit for sins I've committed, wearing my Plato T-shirt, and trying to tell my friend I've failed but I'm still beautiful. Another indulgence: what's failure compared to our nightly discourses ...... with the stars?

I know failure only with respect to love.

I love you Glen and I didn't show that very well. But unless I die tomorrow (God punish the thought) I can damn myself and praise myself enough to believe, to know, that at least we're dealing with the heart.

I'm looking forward to coming back to Toronto now. I decided that I didn't like Corfu during the summer. I tried to not get bothered by the hoards of tourists (they're human beings too, etc.) but the changes are a bit much to really comprehend. Even getting to a crowded beach is a major deal this time of year. So, I hang around the patio and venture into town every once in a while. The Greek tempers are getting a bit shorter as the tourists increase, and it's hot. Winter, with its isolation, cold, and poverty seems attractive from this perspective. There's also a couple of things I'd like to try in Toronto. I think I may have mentioned that we'll be back Aug. 18, just a month from now. We'll be leaving here in the first few days of August, for London, to stay with a wealthy friend of J's, and from there we'll go to Paris for our flight.

J. is one of the most amazing people I've ever met, one of the most understanding and sympathetic (in the real sense of the word). But even so we still have our problems. I'm beginning to get the feeling that I'm a very difficult person to live with.

Sometimes I think the problem is we understand each other a little _too_ well. She's the first woman I can really talk to, and that still catches me by surprise now and then. Then again I know that love is unknowable. But at least I'm beginning to feel that we will win, that the dreamers with the exposed hearts will soon see how well they're really doing.

Apologies for the convulsions in this letter – we'll be able to talk together soon. There's a lot I want to listen to in you – you shine a lot more than you think. There's so much I want to learn from you, and I think I'm beginning to find out how to listen.

God bless you. With much love,

Saro.

To Lis Jakobsen

Day after Labour Day, 1995

Hey, you sweet gods-contested one –

Just in case you've forgotten, it's worth reminding you that each and every god on Olympus – with no exception, not even for the hardly known, silent ones – has taken immutable sides over you. They are still scheming, arguing, and conniving over you. There's a whole lot of eternal fussing, fretting and fighting over you, not because you're so dangerous for them, but because they've let such a bright, lovely, kind, and potato-enhanced wonder to slip by them. Half of them feel inconsolably foolish to have allowed a mere mortal to pose such a serious challenge to their godly ways, while the other half would rather exalt in their liberalness. Apollo (that old stick in the mud), for example, is immortally pissed-off, and Artemis (not to mention Hera) is gloating all the way from Parnassus to Pittsburg. If you cared about all the machinations and turmoil that you, Lis Dalberg Jakobsen of Arhus, cause in the heavens, you'd be even more than the Queen of the Block, even more than the Empress of the Annex.

That's your fate, to be a hassle for heaven. (As for me, it's very straightforward – the Olympians like me and there's no fuss. The rule, that the mad should be favoured – because "those whom the gods would destroy, they first make mad" – is too obvious for them to even think about.)

I'm not being particularly mad in telling you all this. I just wanted to explain why I missed you so much, to see you stroking and rubbing your face again, to see you conquering all that hard, nasty stuff of the last ten months, to realize that you'll always be a pain in the neck to the gods. It makes me sillier, more grateful, and happier.

With the whole splendid catastrophe of the full Lisuccia back, I think I'll remember better and maybe keep myself from falling into those dark pits as often as I used to – perhaps even have the confidence and courage to write for you, even though you're "soft as a prayer and sharp as a knife" and I'm essentially just a dog. I do love you, Lisuccia.

Love,

Saro

5:00 a.m. Mon. Dec. 15 [1998]

Hey you Lisuccia!
("La più bella di tutte le belle" is still your most suitable epithet)

Thanks for taking care of me so well – I know how well you look after me by the feeling of freedom, the steady retreat of the tides of anxiety and sadness that begins with a look in your eye or your hand on my wrist. In no time my heart stops its senseless race to nowhere, the sadness evaporates like morning dew, and I realize that once again your heart has led me out of the hole in the ground to a place where I can stand and feel the sunshine on my face, my old self-respect taking up its lodgings in my heart again.

Like the well-prepared husband in the waiting room, who begins to doubt that his exhortations to breathe, breathe, are helping much in the bloody agony he sees in front of him, and therefore can't help fainting and has to be ministered to while he's still trying to "help" his wife with the delivery – that's a gentle analogy of how I felt this afternoon when I knew I <u>had</u> to go to bed.

And still, the part of me that's still innocent (or naïve – it doesn't matter) tries to assure me that when you're taking care of me, I'm also taking care of you. I know this in my bones, I see it from the other side too. Because when it looks like I'm looking after you, it is really you doing the greater caring, the greater caring of allowing and accepting, even cherishing who I am, the greater caring of putting aside your own personal battles with "self-sufficiency" and "trust" and "faith" to clear the way for the greater dignity of acceptance, particularly the acceptance at love's attempts at work and nurture.

Unfortunately, love's job description is not very clear, and its work often becomes a tangled mess of inefficiency that doesn't seem to achieve much more than an awkward presence, despite the fervor and the passion. And at that point it's you, Lissy Jakobsen, who says, "there, there, we'll undo these knots and tangles after you've had some good sleep – don't you worry."

I hope I haven't been just nervously going on about the obvious again. I never felt this much affection, friendship, good wishes, admiration, love, magic, and closeness. With each passing year those words don't seem to be enough anymore, maybe because we're crossing that even rarer and even holier stream of magic where we find our humanity and our fulfilment in each other's happiness and well-being, – not because we've given up on our individual selves, but because we're beginning to see the truth of the greater magic: that your happiness, well-being, strength and kindness (even beauty) are my happiness and strength and beauty – because we both create them for each other.

You've done all this – and more – for me. And even though my basic nature will never change, because of what you've done, even through the drug days and the horrendously depressed days, I've never felt as close to the world around me and as close to my own skin as I have in the past nine years. You made it possible, you made sure, that I would live the life I have, the one that's really mine, no matter how odd it might seem in the general world that you have always had to continue dealing with.

So I'll close this note with the beginning: Thanks for taking care of me so well, Lissy.

> With you always, and caring,
>
> Tuo marito (still potso – but in a much
> finer way after all these years)   (*)

---

* Saro's humorous misspelling (apparently) of the Italian word *pazzo*, "crazy."

[written up the left margin:]

Could you please get me up before noon. I'd like to take you for lunch and a view or two of an art gallery.

1:00 a.m. [1999]

Dear Lissie,

Both of us have been skirting around edges and walking on
eggshells lately. I'm writing you this note tonight to try to make
it clear that it is not you who has littered the floor with all this
brittleness. Almost all of them, the ones you step lightly around
and the ones I try to soft-shoe through, are mine. Bathetic as it
sounds, they're the broken pieces of myself. That's a country-
and-western kind of way of summing up depression. Depression,
in the days when it was still talked about in other than bio-
chemical terms, likes to alternate between ingratiation and
aggression. Ingratiation (sometimes more kindly termed
generosity and sensitivity) to try to get the constant flow of love
and approval that low self-esteem requires; aggression
(sometimes more kindly termed self-assertion) to avoid the rage
of despair when there is danger that the flow may be cut off. [. . .]

I don't like these pre-biochemical terms because while being very
good at describing depression, they close the door to any hope of
conquering it. In other words, depression is depression because
all the love and approval in the world wouldn't be enough to
satisfy it.

I'm not comfortable with the psychoanalytic description, but that
doesn't mean it's not an accurate picture. [. . .]

I don't mean to bring all the problems we've been experiencing
lately back to me alone. I just wanted to let you know that even
within the lousy confines of depression there are moments, many
moments like now, when I see you. And when I see you I know
that these scenarios are not of your making. I've littered the
ground with broken pieces of myself and you've had to be very
careful. It's a situation I would like to stop – perhaps we can't just

sweep them all away, but I could encourage you to take more chances, especially if I could show, with less contrariness, I hope, that you are the provider, not the destroyer, of a world of love.

I wish I could have put this in one simple sentence, but it's even more complicated than I myself admit. This much though, is simply true: there's still a part of me, a place in the soul or the heart, that belongs more to infinity than analysis, that loves you now and will love you forever, unequivocally, unconditionally, any way you look at it, because of the simple grace and beauty and kindness that comes from inside you into almost everything you do.

Crazy but true,

Saro

Would you like to talk about these things over dinner tonight – perhaps at the Satay?

FICTION

The Feast of St. Joseph
(Edited by Antonino Mazza)

Fascinating fire. Fascinating rhythm. In the name of the Fire and of the Song and of the Holy Smoke. This one isn't even scary. Just the thing when you have the time to see yourself getting older. I know and you know and you know that I know it's not the same fire that burns houses down. This one is downright cozy, as cozy as cozy gets. *Così fan tutte.* Mozart oh Mozart, master of the B-flat fart, darling of the Beaux Arts, don't leave me stranded with your tinkle tinkle in front of an old man's hearth. Come Bach, come fervour just once more, come cozy fun and Tootie. Who you kidding, old man? This fire speaksa the good English. No Calabrian blues. It's a Canadian, well-mannered fire. No chilblains on the shin bones connected to the thigh bones, and so I can't be branded (ha ha) the rounder that I am. All these little flames licking straight up at nothing. And it hardly gives off any heat. God, just for you I stay too drunk to really know. *God said to Abraham kill me a son.* Maybe the chimney draws too well. It takes the heat away with the smoke. Just like Canada: it works too well for its own good. The baby along with the bathwater. *Abe said Man, you must be putting me on.* Soooo Dante (or is it Milton), if Hell is heat without light, this must be heaven I'm in. *Heaven, I'm in heaven and my heart beats so.* Domenico Bizzo. Bizzo, Bizzo, I wonder what ever happened to Bizzo? Bizza me is what his wife used to say. And he did too. Why am I here and you wherever you are? Beatsa me, Bizzo. *God said No, Abe said What.* I shouldn't have had that last cognac. Shouldn't have lost the lottery either. But what the hell, I'm in heaven and my cheeks burn from God's enduring kisses. *When he kisses me I stay kissed.* My son says the soul of America is in an old blues: *everybody wants to get to heaven but nobody wants to die.* I don't care. I'm singing at the feet of my Lord and all is forgiven. And monks make the best cognac. So imagine the cognac in heaven. *God said Abe, you can do anything you want to but the next time you see me coming you better run.* Mary said to

Joseph, "Mon mari, c'est le pigeon!" If Tennessee Williams spoke Neapolitan or some Calabrian dialect, there would be no doubt that I am brilliant. I could have had class, I could have been a pretender, instead of a school janitor, which is what I am. But the kids would have got Tennessee too, in the back streets of Naples, maybe Rome, just like Pasolini. Whosoever lives by the word, dies by the word. *Abe said Where do you want this killing done?* But why is the word so close to the genitals? Oh Tennessee, oh Soren, weren't we erotic enough?

Suddenly last summer, Luca "Tennessee" Tempesta went to heaven without dying. Without ingesting, injecting, or inhaling anything. Without making any movies and without being hopelessly in love with a street urchin. All he did was find himself an apartment with a fireplace, retire, and read a hundred books that told him he was hornier than he would ever know. Imagine Abraham's hard on. Imagine how happy Sarah was, so happy she got an *h* on the end of her name to commemorate forever how her husband's cock pointed straight up to the sky. And just because I'd tell God to fuck himself if he asked me to kill my son I'll never become the father of my people. The true blue chronically flaccid schlong of our times. Gets you to work on time, but that's about it.

And I worked and I worked and I was supposed to keep on working until all the *h*'s dropped off all the Sarahs and my children would put me in an old age home because I didn't kill them for God, an Italian old age home, where I would be happier because they have espresso there and serve wine with the meals and probably wouldn't arrest you if you pinched the nurse's bum. And when I died everybody would remember how hard I worked and how I didn't kill my children and there would be no need to hire professional mourners the way they used to when they buried the ones who hadn't worked too much, the nobles and the priests and the piazza bums. I could have had class if we weren't starving. I was just an ordinary starving young man, accumulating indulgences instead of scout badges. And even as a man, *a man*, dear Lord, I went out and gathered wood and washed the clothes in the river when my mother was in labour. I left in the middle of the night and got back before dawn so no one would see me, so no one could blight our fine family name. It should have been spring but that March was colder than winter. I tripped over a stone and I fell into the brambles beside the path and I tore my clothes and my skin. God how I cursed you that cold cold night. And it still meant something then to bring you and all your saints down and call your mother a whore. And there's something to it, isn't there? I mean, a pigeon? I was even more stupid then. I didn't realize that God understood only the Latin tongue. There wasn't even a ruffle of wind to answer me. And the baby died, like almost all the others that cruel spring.

The English think of heaven as a whorehouse where you can screw forever and still be a virgin. For me it's a hearth with an endless supply of wood, the freedom to change your middle name every night, where you can sit forever and not get chilblains. Tonight I am Burroughs from Tennessee, in heaven. I have running water – hot and cold running water – in three different places in my apartment. Not even Father Gianni ever got that extravagant about heaven. He told us there was a lot of bread to feed the babies and huge wheels of cheese and cherry trees that brought forth fruit three times a year. And to help me get there he gave me ten or a hundred Our Fathers and Hail Marys. The stubbed feet and torn skin were not enough.

"That's just the flesh, my son."

Just like your whore, I wanted to say. But I didn't have the freedom of a middle name then.

"I swore, Father." "Whom did you blaspheme and how many times?"

"God, his mother, and all the saints. Twice."

"Have you committed any other sins? Sins against the flesh? For sins against the flesh are also sins against God."

"Someone heard me, Father."

"Heard you touching?"

"No, someone heard me swearing in the brambles. It was the feast of St. Joseph. I thought he was trying to warn me."

"I'm sure St. Joseph will intercede for you."

"He didn't, my brother was born dead. God made him born dead."

"Or maybe he was alive until the moment you cursed the Heavens. Maybe he died exactly when you despaired and cursed God. It's not for nothing that swearing is considered momentary despair and therefore a mortal sin. And maybe this is all a blessing for you, a gift of God's wisdom, a chance to really see the light." The fortunate fall again. It was a dark moonless night. I didn't buy it, not even then.

"I guess I shouldn't forget that I did touch myself."

"How many times?" asked Father Gianni absently.

"Twice. No, six times. And somebody touched me too."

"Was it the team effort after the Sunday game at the Santissimo? I hear about it almost every week. Eight or nine of you in a circle touching yourselves and trying to synchronize the spilling of your seed. Calabria's answer to the Roman fountains."

"No, Father, it wasn't a boy who touched me. I couldn't play soccer last Sunday because we're still in mourning. It was a woman."

"Don't tell me you've already started going to the Bella Elena? Poor woman. As though she didn't have enough troubles."

"She also has many indulgences. You know she doesn't take boys under eighteen. Why do you give her so many indulgences? She already has over four thousand years. I go on every pilgrimage, carry an emblem in every procession, assist you at Mass once a month, say my prayers every night, and even with kissing St. Nicholas' toe as often as I can, at last count I had 202 years of indulgences. Is it fair that an altar boy has two hundred while a whore has four thousand?"

"Perhaps she'll need them more than you will. But you're here to confess, not theologize. Where did the woman touch you?"

"On my thing."

"No, Luca, I mean where were you?"

I bet you did, Gianni. As if we couldn't hear the dainty little grunts that come from behind the screen after the stories of our team efforts. It didn't really sound like a cough at all. There was no need to say excuse me, go on.

"It was the night of the feast of St. Joseph, Father. I was out gathering wood because my mother was in labour. It was very cold and we needed more wood for the fireplace. I was carrying a heavy faggot and I stumbled over some stones, stubbed my foot and fell into the brambles beside the path. That's when I started swearing. I didn't want to be late. I didn't want the baby to get cold. Then I heard a woman's voice from further up the path, from that small olive grove in Don Sebastiano's land, the one overlooking the river opposite the cemetery bank."

"Yes, I know the damned place, the famous Seduction Grove, where any woman who's ever been with child and unmarried still blames Pan or some mysterious, intoxicating music in the olive trees for her immaculate conception."

"But Father, Pan can take the form of a dove, can't he?" Poor St. Joseph, heard the same story himself. And I confess, dear Lord, that I still don't know why the village didn't have a hundred Christs. There's so much you can do with piety if you just take it out of the churches and into the streets. I knew even then that if I could kill my unborn brother with a few curses I could do much more with a little piety.

Smoke started to waft through the screen. Nazionale, ten lire each, but I knew he would say it was the tin can he used as a brazier under his soutane if I asked him for a drag. Father Gianni was obviously settling down to another Seduction Grove story and maybe thinking of Filomena, his full-figured housekeeper. God turned a blind eye to the extra duties she performed, perhaps because in his wisdom this was small compensation for the difficult journey Father Gianni had chosen. After all, no one forced him to go to the land that God forgot. He could have stayed in Rome and become a bishop. The whole village knew he was on familiar *tu* terms with members of the Curia. With others, the form of address could be a sticky problem. The new official form of polite address was *Lei* but fascists showed their allegiance to the peninsula's ancient glories by still using the old form, *Voi*. And the Vatican had just signed the Concordat with Mussolini. In delicate matters, they resorted to Latin, still another step up in formality, but less fraught with danger.

"Well, to make a long story short, Father, the woman asked if I was hurt and I pretended I was stuck and bleeding in the brambles. As she started to disentangle me I took my Pan pipes out of my pocket and started playing a tune that never failed to bring my four goats back from wherever they were. I should confess Father, that in that still, moonless night, the coldest St. Joseph's that anyone can remember, when the frozen dew on the high oaks and the still small-leafed walnut trees framed the multiplying stars..."

"Luca, you're not here to give me one of your famous recitations," Gianni snapped. "This is the house of God and you are here to be absolved of your sins if you are truly sorry for them. But you don't sound repentant in the least. Will you confess your sins and will you atone?"

"Father, it's not easy."

"I know it's hard, son," and I know His Randiness wondered if he had chosen the wrong word, for there was a slight pause and Father Gianni was not known to pause, "and that's why I'm here, to assure you of God's promise that there is no sin horrendous enough not to be forgiven if you are truly sorry. It is said that there is more joy in heaven..."

"Then heaven should be cracking up by now," I burst in, "because it was Filomena, your Filomena, who bent down to disentangle me and grabbed my thing instead and squeezed with both her hands and kissed it and put it in her mouth and sucked on it like her life depended on it and lifted her skirts and fell back against a gnarled olive trunk and let go of my huge hard thing just long enough to throw her legs around my waist and pull me against her where it made its way like lightning because she was dripping wet right down to her bare feet and I'm not poeticizing either."

This time the pause was longer. There was no more smoke coming through the grille. Shadows darted across the screen, just like bats after sunset in Tennessee. He must have been crossing himself furiously. No, that would have been old Father Genio. Father Gianni must have been dusting the cigarette ash off his sleeve, composing himself, casually, with rapid flicks of long white fingers: an aristocratic flutter of the hand performed ceremoniously by all the titled men of the village. Sometimes in the piazza they formed semi-circles of draped figures, jackets slung over their shoulders with the sleeves empty, punctuating points with an eloquent wave of the hand and the jackets never slid off their shoulders. This was one of nobility's many mysteries, though some of the peasants believed that the jackets were pinned to the shirts at the shoulder. Some of them continued to believe this even after Ruthless Sevenglasses and the Notable Shitdragger, on a dare, brushed against an illustrious semi-circle and knocked two of the miracle jackets off. And despite the clamour of obsequious mutterings in the best peasant style, Sevenglasses and Shitdragger never again worked the gentry's groves or used the marchese's mill. To his credit, Father Gianni was never quite comfortable in those semi-circles and he never grew his little fingernail long the way his peers did. Nonetheless, I took out my knife and opened it.

The long pause was finally interrupted by the squeak of the grille slowly opening. It was almost imperceptible, but it was opening and I poised my knife over it. Father Gianni coughed and began to speak, quietly and evenly.

"Poetry is one thing, but vicious lies are another, and liars, worst of all, go to the very centre of Hell."

"And where do cuckolds go, Father? To Limbo, like dead babies?"

The grille flew open and his long thin fingers grabbed my neck. I stabbed at them twice (I was thinking of my next confession, I remember the number) and I scrambled across the pew and ran down the nave of the dark church and crouched down behind the last pew, ears pricked (oh my English) waiting for the tirade of goddamn and whoreson and *vigliacco*, coward, the most putrescent utterance in all Calabrian. So that there is no mistake about it, it is one of a handful of words that never changes from dialect to dialect in all of Italy – it is just about the only thing we all agree on. I waited in the special darkness of a Calabrian church (there is nothing darker), a darkness inherited from Norman gloom (qu'est-ce que nous faisons ici où on chante trop et on pleure encore plus) and for all I know, from Norman Douglas's dark visits to these unknown parts (Douglas will be my middle name tomorrow night) in search of ever more exotic little boy bums ("perhaps the greatest travel writer since Pausanias"). No one can swear like a priest, and rightly so.

Mary help us all. I must be getting sober. One more cognac, a double or so, one for the maybe and one more for the load. No, the tirade never came, just a whimpering in the Norman darkness and some mutterings in Latin. I wonder how the good Father would have fared after Vatican II? At least I would have understood what he was whimpering about that night. Dear Father Gianni, I am writing to you from Canada (yes, I too thought I was going to America) after all these years because my conscience will not be assuaged for the shameful sin I committed in your confessional forty years ago today, St. Joseph's (and I thought it was a cold one then) when I was a young lad full of mischief and you were a young priest full of piety. I can say it now because we are both full of age. I am not sure if the Church allows confessions by mail, but I hope you will read my story and forgive my sin, for I am old enough now to be truly sorry. It was forty years ago today, the coldest St. Joseph's ever, until I came to Canada. You used to hear confessions on Saturday evenings from people coming back from the fields. For forty years I have hoped that the magnanimity of your heart has relegated the incident I am about to relate to the Pit of Excrement where it belongs. (You may recall that the Pit of Excrement was filled in by the Americans as part of the Marshall Plan after the war. Do the goats still use the modern lavatories they built? Forgive me, I digress, as I have always done. Nor should I presume that you would know such things. You left the village even before I did.) It was forty years ago today that I lied to you and to God in the sanctity of the confessional, all because I knew it would bring laughter on evenings when me and my friends had completed our customary double circuit of the village and it was still, still too hot or too cold or too still or too sad or too beautiful to go home. All of us should have become great drunks, but I am the only one who succeeded. It became part of the rich history of our village, taking its place next to Donna De Luna's decapitation at the hands of Sevenglasses and Shitdragger who used her head to make a scarecrow in the piazza, at Don Sebastiano's gate, a black jacket pinned at the shoulders. That was the real history, not the incomprehensible nonsense that Don Nicola wrote in the rarefied Italian of the North, as if our village really were just the product of Bourbon intrigue, Norman rudeness, French tyranny, Albanian pollution, and distant pulses of splendid Rome and sublime Greece. The real history polished the village stone and seeped its way into every child's blood as magic, as the enchantment of possibility (anyone could grow up to cut off a noble head). The low walls at the bottom of our steep streets may well have been built by the Normans to stop the torrents of water that gushed down during the endless rains of winter, but in reality they marked a vast labyrinth that not even the lizards knew, labyrinths that led to openings where, if you followed the dream in every detail, treasures could be found. I have read our nobleman's history and I have read even the American and French anthropologists who turned to Calabria when the exotic tribes started dwindling and found a persistence of treasure hoard myths and clan-endorsed vendettas. Poor us, the lessons of Aeschylus never reached us. I do not deny their science, but we have the same word for poetry and science in the less refined language of our village.

Forgive me, I am presuming again. Of my village. Don't poets and scientists both deal with possibility? Scientists have managed to make our lives immeasurably easier, in this part of the world at least, by denying one possibility, the possibility of sin, the possibility of evil. And that's why a brilliant seminarian such as yourself chose to work among the humble and the ignorant. Where would you have gone if there were no Calabria? You stayed with us because you knew we still believed in evil. What you hadn't counted on was that we believed in evil more than in salvation. Your suffering must have been immense. How deeply you must have been moved the first time you saw our Good Friday procession and realized that the flagellants' chains were meant to make more than an awesome rattle and that the crowns of thorns we wore behind the raised statue of the crucified Christ did not have the inside thorns removed. The blood was real, bubbling with real possibilities. Donna De Luna's head in the piazza was real, another true emblem of belief. How long did it take for you to see that the South doesn't have symbolic levels of actuality, or that we don't make much of a distinction between the literal and the symbolic. How long was it before our strident landscape pulled you down to the level of skin and bones and incomprehensible seasons, how long was it before you exchanged the venialities of the poor mind for the mortal sins of the body? Filomena knew her part in the landscape and slowly, you began to know too. How delicious a moment it must have been when you realized you were one of us, when you stopped speaking to God in Latin. Did you feel awkward trying to pray to him in the Venetian dialect you grew up with, the one you thought you had forgotten, the one that sounded so strange without the canals and pretty glass? Did you know we had the same problem, never knowing whether God listened better when we spoke our own language or, as we all suspected, he found our tongue as incomprehensible as you did at first. Did you know that that was why you could never get us to give up our so-called superstitions? God doesn't speak dialects and only the titled ones had any ease with Standard Italian. Do you see now why we believed more in votives of little tin legs or eyes than in heartfelt prayers? Our Hail Marys and Our Fathers were magic incantations, not because we are a clannish, landrooted people but simply because we had no idea of what the words meant. And I guess it takes old age and a perverse urge to settle scores to make me see that this is true of more than prayers: I tell you I feel the same way about my own children. So, tonight, I confess to you Father, in Standard Italian, that I slandered your good name for the sake of adding something ominous to the night and with my friends, for the sake of lingering on together after we had already made our double circuit of the village and the moon was high and we were sharing a cigarette that one of us had bought or stolen and for a while nobody was dying or hungry and the stars were twinkling just as they always did and we were all kings of the village. Father, I'm sorry if you thought my lies were an attempt to settle scores for your insinuating me into my brother's death. The real reason for my lies, as you probably know by now, was just to create good stories to share with my friends on starry nights. I confess that even in my old age I don't know of any other reason to act. I have raised three children in order to manufacture stories for my old age. And what a terrible job they're doing in this story-impoverished part of the world. Remember what the women used to say: it's better to raise pigs than children – you can slaughter the pigs but there's no gain in offspring. They never heard of Abraham and Isaac and they don't need stories as much as we do. I confess that your suicide that evening did much to enrich, if not immortalize my story, and that I would have not run away from the village if Filomena hadn't found you hanging in the apse, swinging from the altar to the pulpit. I didn't know then how well you had learned the lessons of the village; I really thought you were dead. Perhaps after failing in Jonestown you became a Graham Greene whiskey priest in El Salvador or Guatemala where you finally understood that the paradox between God's love for his people and his disdain for incomprehensible languages allows you to ignore the Pope and carry a gun under your soutaine. Perhaps you have even discovered the exotic psychedelia of those regions and know that Jesus is among us once more, this time as Ricardo Montalban drinking black coffee in a white suit. So, I shall address this letter care of his studio in Hollywood and hope it reaches you eventually. I must sign off now. I am almost sober. Yours in Christ and in all his wonders, Luca.

Maria

(Edited by Antonino Mazza)

I like Jacques Cousteau.

I like the idea of an old man in a wetsuit falling backwards into mother sea.

There's something about that mystery fish he's obsessed with, the one that no one or nothing has ever seen, swimming through a black cavern in a black void, eyeless and oblivious to any rumour of light. Especially on a night like this. It stirs something deep inside you. Or perhaps it's just the remarkable production values that M. Cousteau demands everywhere the *Calypso* takes him. In any case, you sit up in your chair as he gets closer. The angels come to attention and something quickens in your heart. You recall your youth and, finally, you can resume eating your sandwich with a clear conscience again.

I like to see him busy on board, too, bent over a bank of blue screens, sonar, oscillators and other intricately subtle instruments to plot movements and plumb depths and reveal more fish than are dreamed of in our philosophy.

And he certainly knows that when the signal fires announcing the fall of Troy skipped across the wine-dark Aegean many were the fish that leapt and danced in the molten gold and violet waters, quickening the heart of Clytemnestra and scaring the shit out of Aegisthus, her stay-at-home lover. That too, I like.

To this day there are fish that still dance in the moonlit waters of Marechiare, especially when the fishermen venture out onto that postcard bay with a lantern on the bow and a black banner on a mast of reeds and sing the old Neapolitan songs, though for Jacques Cousteau these are only misty, shrouded memories of long-ago student days.

Even down below, where he has poured himself a cup of coffee and is now lighting a Gitane, he remains resolute. I think it is a Gallic attitude he strikes, sitting at the little galley table, chin cupped in hands, smoke from his fingers curling through his hair while he gazes at the little Polaroid of his family taped to the hull, not regretting, even for a minute, that it's women and children who go first.

I like these moments, and shall return, God willing, to share his smoky depths a while longer.

It's just that it's never very long before the wailing of an ambulance tears through the underwater silence of these late nights and drags the tragic chorus of the Trojan women in its wake.

It's Aeschylus on the graveyard shift again, making his usual rounds of the all-night convenience stores and hospital waiting rooms, handing out consolation and condolence along with handbills for his latest tragedy.

I like the idea of an old man with a stack of fliers and a staple gun tacking up the word on necessity and fate and how it can work for you. In the sad night. He leans across the counter of the empty 7-Eleven and whispers in the ear of the turbaned clerk. Just one look, he is saying slowly and clearly, just one look at the pitying masks of my intractable chorus and you know, I mean you can feel it in your bones, that man grows wise against his will. Then he straightens himself out a bit, and asks, more casually, who won the game and if they carry foreign cigarettes. No? It doesn't matter, I'll have a large package of Export Plain. And cheer up. So what if Agamemnon never got the chance to regret treading on the purple and putting the torch to his daughter on the pyre. Tough titty for him. The powers above by ruthlessness commend their love, you know.

There are some unpleasant truths the old guy has to tell. There's no denying you can beat your breasts and tear your hair out and make all the precise and exemplary sacrifices and still not get a straight answer from the gods.

That's because it was man who taught the gods to speak, the store clerk wanted to say. But he thought better of it. It was a heresy even in Titan times, and besides, despite the tough guy stance, he could tell that the old geezer really did feel for us. I myself know for a fact that when he goes on break and finds himself sitting alone with a can of pop in some desolate corner of a hospital cafeteria, maybe re-reading the warning on his cigarette package, he catches himself wishing that the truth were lies and torments himself with the outrageous possibility of naming them love, whether agape or eros, perhaps some new goddess would decide.

These are the moments I would like to attend to in the quickly fading light, the moments I could spend the whole night trying. But I can't fool myself as well as I used to and can't pretend that I've really forgotten how the whole sad affair wound up.

Achilles fought against his will, Troy was sacked and burned to the ground and my wife died shortly after Helen.

And Aeschylus, poor Aeschylus, holding back the tears in some infinitely inconsolable corner of an emergency waiting room, never lived to see it, could hardly have imagined it, that the gods would eventually begin to regret what they had done to man and end up nailing their true begotten son to a cross just to prove how sorry they were.

Perhaps there's nothing more to be said, but an old man must keep pretending, if daybreak is going to mean anything at all, if there's any difference between dying in your sleep and having an espresso in the morning. There must be something to say tonight about the bottle of wine beside me, about the adamant underwater men, the born-again witness just now reminiscing about his former godless life of drugs and unemployment on the late-night salvation show, this bemused flicker of something I used to call fear as I pick a flea off my wrist and find myself wondering if fleas can carry AIDS as well as the Black Plague, the silence that resounds from the room upstairs where the young man coughed all night for a month and a half until he died in his lover's arms without asking for forgiveness from his parents who would rather have lost an arm than have a homo son, and every night I wanted to say a prayer and didn't know what to pray for and couldn't take the chance, for the young man's sake. But still, there must be something left to say, even though god can manage to be ruthless enough without my intervention.

Still, the new fish is inevitable, the next step already here. Another glass of wine then, another stab at what is possible, one more version of the story for the night.

Tonight it's not the courage of underwater men I want to fathom, not the depths of God's regrets (his precious apologies became tedious long ago), but just to see if the ending of a story makes any sense of the beginning, just to see if at the end it turns out I was the stand-in or the passer-by or the hero or the villain of the tale, not to find justification or meaning, but just to know, like a child learning a new game, if the first tries really count. Not to drink for nothing, in other words, and dodder through what's left, regrets in hand, appraising the geometry of the stars and dispensing explanations for what happened, excuses for what didn't.

I was just following orders.

We were too hungry to know any better.

They took me prisoner to a cold country far away.

I turned back at the foot of the village and never went home again.

If you didn't know your part, if you didn't save the damsel in distress, if you stood helplessly and watched your child die, if you didn't stop the holocaust, if you ate your sandwich while others starved, you end up giving your children reasons instead of faith, theology instead of hope. Very skinny words, these, even in my native tongue.

I didn't rescue the maiden. I watched my child starve. I didn't stop the holocaust. But tonight I'll try the story again and drink enough to make it matter and understand how both the good guys and the bad guys are deceived into winning.

I think I started out as a good guy, or at least I bought the story about the son on the cross and how sorry his father was.

Don Ignazio, on the other hand, was definitely one of the bad guys. I mean, his tragic flaw was worse than mine.

With a beautiful wife, I was a Menelaus kind of guy, auburn hair, not abnormally stupid, just off somewhere else when it happened. And, naturally, Don Ignazio had to be a Paris kind of man, devoted to beauty and fated to steal a famous bride. Unlike Paris though, Don Ignazio's looks weren't anything for the goddesses to fight over. I've learned in my new life that this is the kind of detail, credible and particular, that Aeschylus and other dramatists overlooked in their golden age that is essential to our more dynamic times. We say he longed for the beauty that was never his; Aeschylus says he was born to raise hell.

When the messenger caught up with me at the railway station in Sant'Eufemia to tell me my wife was dead, he grabbed both my arms with his giant hands, squeezed them tightly, buried his head in my shoulder, and cried like a baby. Perhaps it would have been awkward even if he wasn't half a foot taller than me, even if my narrow shoulders could more easily support the heaving of his massive head and chest with every sob.

"Maybe now they'll take some notice," he tried to blurt out between the heaving and the sobbing, his onerous task compounded by his commendable attempt to inform me of the tragedy in the proper Tuscan tongue, as befitting the gravity and solemnity of the occasion and in deference to them, the gods and all the powers that be, who were sure to take offence at our southern dialect. Of course nowadays, with our new philosophy and hundreds of linguists and philologists from the northern universities scouring the hills and mountains of the South with tape recorders, we no longer point the finger at fate. We know now that the real tragedy is language and we look instead toward the silent fish, the distant speechless planets, the old woman in a remote village on the crest of the mountain in Calabria who is the last person on earth who knows the name of the little yellow and orange flowers that used to grow near the trunks of the loquat trees in the higher terraces.

Finally, he looked up at the station ceiling and implored the gods directly, as properly as he could, giving me the chance to drop my head on his chest. And I too wanted to cry like a baby, but the tangle of dialect and Italian words that squirmed and knotted themselves together in my skull and in my chest found no way out and I had no tears to break the absurdity. All I could manage was the strange believing and unbelieving *no no no* which, fortuitously enough, is the same in both the vulgar and genteel tongues.

Forty-three years later I have a better understanding of these things and I can say, simply, it's not the way it should have happened. When they bring you the news of your wife's death it should be in the vernacular, not merely because the world has become much less formal these days, but just to ease up on our penchant for the maudlin and bathetic.

Now I know how to act when they bring you the news of your wife's death. You should not be muttering on a larger man's chest. You should be standing alone, solidly, motionless and silent, with your gaze frozen on something in midair, while the messenger, courageous beneath his stoic appearance, like a good doctor on TV, shatters the unbearable despair into manageable pieces with some well-chosen, informal, pithy words that you know you will recall, with strength and gratitude, when life tries you again.

Then you lift your gaze slowly skyward and realize that the seemingly imperturbable little clouds of summer are giving themselves away by drifting a little higher in the sky than usual for that time of year. A reversal of the flag at half-mast, you should think. But I was young, and a peasant, and didn't know the protocol for such things.

After a while, my whole body collapsed under the weight of starched Italian and shameful dialect and I began to cry and couldn't stop. And we cried our hearts out in the station, Ettore and I, and no one was alarmed.

Sant'Eufemia was known as another station of the cross from the day it was built. It was a common enough sight. In fact, it was pretty well all you saw in the railway station. Men huddling with their children or hugging their mothers and their fathers for as long as they could before taking that awesome step onto the train that would take them to war or to America, Australia or Argentina, mothers still desperately commending their children to God long after the train had disappeared from the tracks, some anxious to return with pockets full of money, others secretly elated to be almost gone.

When our sobbing subsided enough we started on our way home, Ettore and I, on the steady climb from the ribbon of the coast that the tracks sketched out, up through the terraced hills to the skirts of the mountains. By now the *no no no* had devoured everything I ever held inside me, yet the world, the mountains and the villages huddled against them, the valleys with their roaring torrents, each flower and fruit tree, looked and felt and sounded and smelled exactly the same as before. As though my wife weren't dead. As though I hadn't been away for seven years. As though she was dead for nothing, I later learned to add.

With the wisdom of hindsight, if not age, I know it should have been six years or eight years that I had been away, not that clichéd seven. It cheapens your story to have such obviously portentous numbers punctuating your life. It reduces your life to grammar — of English or Italian, of the cosmos or the Holy One, but grammar nonetheless. Not that grammar and numbers and the music of the spheres are without charm. I like the idea of old men measuring the celestial distances in thirds and fifths and sevenths and listening for the chords that stretch across the universe. I like to think of teams of mathematicians bent over a bank of blue screens and immensely powerful computers plumbing the void to unveil the greatest prime number. After years of relentless searching, an almost inconceivably long and glaringly precise figure finally rolls through the screens and we catch it in the Sunday paper. And years later it will be vital in the discovery of darker underwater caves, essential for sending spaceships to black planets.

But the facts, cheap as they are, are still the facts, and it was an even seven years that I had been away. And still, the chalk grey villages pasted on the mountainsides in front of me looked exactly the same. Calami, Scoppio, Filadema, San Dionisio, still clinging to the mountains, tempting fate and gravity. But I didn't know about Aeschylus then, nor, now that I think about it, about gravity. And like the rest of the peasants from the timeless, unchanging villages, all I could read was some simple sentences in the stars and a few verbs in the wind and the clouds. It was some prime number of years later that I discovered nostalgia and Newton, immigration and classical tragedy, and a thousand other reasons why the world does not change.

The fig trees charged the air around them with the same dizzying smell of savage green exuberance. I hadn't seen a fig tree for seven years and the air on the path was the same emerald wildness I had tried to remember in Abyssinia and Scotland. When I drink enough it is the same now in my New World room.

The rivers tumbling over the crevices and rushing madly through the steep valleys, they too sounded the same. Unseen, foreboding murmuring in the distance; alluring, fresh, and thunderous as we drew closer. And as the faint rumbling grew slowly, almost imperceptibly, into a low roar, I began to sense my own part in the story, as if I had collaborated somehow, from the very beginnings in a conspiracy of mountains and torrents, sounds and scents, immutability and hope.

It was after many kilometers up the winding paths through the lower terraces when Ettore regained his native speech, if not his composure, and the morass of insane, intoxicating details emerged, one after the other in a terrifying randomness, each galvanized with pathos or utter insignificance and each instrumental, it seemed, in the conspiracy of the landscape. As if each little piece of the mad story had always been there, pristine and timeless, as logical and as senseless as the mountain goat path we were climbing.

She was lying in a pool of blood in the middle of the piazza.

Don Ignazio's shrine will never be finished.

The sky darkened and it started to rain.

It was Sunday.

The earth shifted and moved but there were no landslides.

Everybody in the whole village, even those who hadn't gotten to the piazza yet, screamed for the Madonna or the Saviour according to their family affiliation. Some were actually screaming for both.

The dog's mange was suddenly cured.

Don Ignazio staggered through the crowd in the piazza with half his head blown off.

The rain turned to hail the size of chickpeas and cherries.

He was still holding the shotgun.

Maria's eyes were open in that pool of blood but she looked peaceful and beautiful like a Madonna.

Don Ignazio was blinded by passion.

There were worms coming out of his head.

She never left the house without praying in front of her father's picture.

Don Ignazio's ear was never found.

The sun came out in a flash and all the hailstones melted.

He was blinded by God.

She never left the house without praying in front of your picture, too.

The Ancient One says you can see the fineness of the day in early morning.

Don Ignazio staggered through the crowd and could still speak with only half a head.

We were all so stunned we didn't notice the dog lapping up her blood.

What could I do? What could I do? was all he said.

Father Gianni said she would have forgiven him, but I didn't know if he meant her assassin or the dog.

She was too beautiful to live.

She was too good for this world.

In the South when they die young it is because they were too good or too beautiful to live.

Both, they said, in Maria's case. In the South beauty and goodness are marked for an early heaven. Australia took us and Europe took us and Africa took us and North and South America took us, but we kept our best for heaven. Mothers, especially, begin to worry if their children become too fair or too obedient. Go out and get into some trouble, they say. Don't comb your hair so much. Tell me a dirty joke, and for God's sake, don't be such a saint.

Maria had it coming from the start. A face like an angel's, they'd sigh, a heart as nourishing as bread. And a husband just stupid enough not to do anything about it.

Every morning before leaving the house she stopped in front of the picture of her father in the kitchen. He had died when she was seven months old but she knew him better than anyone alive, in a different way, she said, like Saint Anthony or San Rocco she said, kind quiet men whose faces were filled with heaven, more alive in the frozen love of their pictures and plaster statues than anyone who moves and breathes in this world. She went on the pilgrimages to the places these men protected, walking through the valleys to San Nicola in December, along the streams and rivers to San Giuseppe in March, over the mountains to Vallalta in June, at least one saint and another village every month, and cheered with all of us, her heart as big as the sea, when the bearers heaved the platform onto their shoulders and bore the saint out of the church and into the world.

In the Abruzzi the snake handlers threw serpent after serpent on Saint Dominic in his procession, in Bari they took their San Nicola for an excursion on a rowboat and dumped him into the Adriatic if it didn't rain that year, in Naples everything depended on how quickly the vial of San Gennaro's blood liquefied to a respectable crimson in early May, the Easter of the Roses in all the South, the less critical Whitsunday in the New World.

I was still a POW in Scotland the first time Padre Pio soared into the clouds at Pomigliano just in time to scoop the pilot out of the sky. And it was still many years before I wondered why it was always Italian airmen that he caught in his arms. I'm giving myself away again, but I don't hold it against him. Yes, I too followed the plaster saints and climbed up to the caves that the Mother of God took over from Cybele.

And I too cheered. Cheering never hurts, I think. For Maria, though, it was a less tenuous happiness to have the saint among us.

We married when she was eighteen and struggled through our first year as best we could, which meant the usual thing in the South, hunger and prayer, the death of a child, before resigning yourself to the usual solution. A friend of a relative in Argentina or Canada or Addis Abbaba or Brooklyn or Melbourne would be found to advance the fare. Then came the day you took your first train ride, to the embassy and the medical examination in Rome, and if you didn't have TB and weren't denounced by someone with a grudge to bear, for being a Communist say, or for stealing a rose, you packed your case, embraced your friends and family one last time and took the train again, to Naples and the ship now. And by the second or third week at sea you finally gave in to a strange, new sensation, something like a fear of how far you could really go.

There were letters the first few years, letters I brushed across my face to feel. The words the corporal read to me said she was well and prayed for the day when I returned. It was Sevenglasses, the sacristan, who wrote her letters, half a lira a page, and read her mind.

"Dearest Spouse, I have received your letter of the seventeenth of October 1936 and I am very pleased to learn that you are in good health. I too am in good health, for which I thank God and pray all the time to be reunited again."

That's not the way it should have been. A soldier in a war in a country almost impossibly far away should still hear something in a letter from home. There should be an echo of a human voice, some sounds you know you shared. But even if you knew how to write, the languages of the South were never written and what Sevenglasses and the other scribes knew of the language of the North was lifeless and just as distant.

That's how many of us first realized it was not impossible to forget your family. In any case, Maria's sister had already been abandoned to the dust of a foreign grammar by a husband who found more warmth in the voice of a Toronto woman than in the stilted attempts of his southern wife's best Italian. *Standard Italian and the Abandonment of Families by Calabrian Immigrant Men.*

There must be a paper on it somewhere by now. In any case, I do like the idea of a semiotic deconstruction of his last letter home.

"Dearest Spouse, I have received your letter of the sixth of April 1936 which found me in good health thanks to God. I pray to God that this too finds you in good health and I must inform you that I possess a new family in Canada and therefore it is not possible to send you further communications."

But perhaps distance works both ways. There was never a word about Don Ignazio's initiatives in the letters I received in Africa.

It was because she was a saint and didn't want to add to your suffering, Ettore said. And for years I tried to believe it. It wasn't until I myself learned to read and write that I realized some things are not possible to say. Every month, when she got your money from Africa, Ettore said, the first thing she did was buy the stamps for your letters and put a couple of lire aside for the sacristan. It was only then that she bought the candles for the Virgin and for her father's picture. But she felt badly about the extra expense of the candles and tried to make it up, always looking for other laundry to take to the river, hunting frogs on the sly, even though that's man's work, things like that, and if she couldn't find the extra work, she fasted for a day or two. She was a saint, Ettore said, and now they'll notice.

In our year together she always managed to spare a little olive oil to make a lamp at least. I never tried to stop her, not even when the baby died.

It's common enough by now. It all boils down to a little lump in the throat by this time of night, a deep respect for mercy and the second bottle, especially now that Jacques Cousteau is safely asleep down below and the last tear-filled sinner has opened up his heart to Jesus on the late night salvation show. Soon there won't be any arguments to make about the flame.

Maria knew — we all knew — that the light from a wax candle, five or six times more expensive than the lamp you could make with a little string pierced through a bit of cork or bark in olive oil floating in a glass of water, was more effective and pleasing to the ones above. What would she think now? I haven't tacked her picture to the wall, let alone stuck any kind of flame in front of it. But, if there are still arguments to be made, the imageless wall might not save me either.

The facts, Sal, just the facts.

Yes, every morning before leaving the house she recited the Angelus and prayed for me and her father in front of our pictures on the wall. There were always two lamps or two candles going.

Goodness seemed to run in the family, so when her father was twenty-five a truck fell on top of him. I think the gods got a little sloppy with that one, and had both father and daughter meet their fate at exactly the same age. He was returning home on this same winding road that Ettore and I are climbing, when a truck spun off the third hairpin turn above him, brushed the tops of the loquat trees on the first terrace, the tops of the pomegranates on the second terrace, and landed on his head on the third.

We've left the paths for the road, Ettore and I, edging along the slopes — it takes a year to make one and only a moment to destroy it, the Ancient One said — and we're winding our way through the marchese's terraced fruit groves toward the village I haven't seen in a mythic number of years. We pass the small wrought iron cross that marks the spot where the truck fell on Giovannino Arducci's head and Ettore starts to wail again, in our own language this time, because we're closer to home and it's just for us mortals now.

At last she is with her father, he said. I agreed. For a moment I even felt I wanted to join them, almost giving in to the unspeakable, as though the confusion that had seized my body had quickened into a choice I couldn't recognize, something between crying and being cried over, a choice that immediately hardened into a simple hope that the Ancient One's landslide would push me back to the sea or an earthquake would split the road and swallow me alive. It was just a few moments later, when the earth hadn't budged, when everything remained the same, that I knew the only choice was silence and that my complicity in the intrigues of time and air would remain immutable to the end.

Many years later, after donning my wetsuit and tentatively exploring what lay beneath the waves, I came across a new word, a word that didn't exist in our antique tongue, a word that promised freedom from collusion in those machinations. I discovered guilt, a prime new word, and I could soar away from the mountains, travel to faraway worlds and look back at myself and see the histrionic part I had played in my sorrow, a Mussolini of mourning, bantering about fate and conspiracy and God when there was just guilt and guilt's little reasons.

It wasn't my fault Maria wanted to be a saint. It wasn't my fault Maria was murdered — I wasn't even there.

Heaven is what we invent to justify our illusions.

It is ourselves we mourn for. And I learned how if you start with guilt and diligently pursue its analysis for seven years you will be cured. The old feeling that you are alive because you weren't good enough to die will become just a memory of murkier days. You will accept the reality at the bottom of the ocean and you will be blameless. You will be authorized to do as you see fit and the earth will be your handmaiden. You will be able to use the letter *s* with a clear conscience and enjoy your sandwich in almost any situation.

You will never despair again. You will never wonder if they are together in heaven after all, happy as the day is long, looking down at us and smiling the beatific smile of pity, seeing how hard we're taking it, knowing and not quite being able to say there's no need at all to fuss and fret and feel sorry as we do.

Right up until the last minute we have all the chances in the world. That's how sorry he feels for all he's put us through. Even at the last moment we can regret everything and open our hearts to eternity.

He doesn't up the ante just because he's got you by the balls. Instead, he offers you odds beyond your wildest dreams. These few miserable moments that are left to you against an eternity of easy sevens, full houses, and sitting pat. Just open up your heart and you can start parlaying all those bits of broken dreams into the sure thing of forever. Just say the word and you'll be cashing in at the hundred-dollars-and-up wicket in the entrance to the pearly gates above you.

You hear your heart start to sputter. You look at how fast the little pocket of sand is running through the glass. You see the candle in front of you gasping its last few mouthfuls of air, and you go for it. There will be no one left to blame, nothing left to lose, and an eternity to gain.

But I don't think I'll be fooled again. It's just the final con, the one he trots out for us when we're old and tired and feeling sorry for the young, when everything that's lost is never coming back and all the kitschy contraptions that measure out our lives are creaking to a stop. The sentimental hourglasses and candles, the ticking clocks and tolling bells are only cheap analogues to indulge our sentimental view of things. In heaven his instruments are infinitely more precise, the latest in clean digital equipment and high resolution terminals.

Terminals. I like that. I especially like the fact that you don't get it. I laugh in your face with my own cheap jokes. It is the only thing I have that you can't touch even though there would be no end to the murdering and maiming you would do for it.

With my own laughter I can see right through your little scam. You can't ask me to regret my life because it was never mine to regret. Your son may have bought it, but I'm not going to take the fall for your mistakes.

I laugh at your bogeyman time. He's not fooling me with all that quivering and sniveling at my feet. He's just waiting for his chance to lap up my blood. He doesn't fool me, not yet at least. I down another glass, kick his skinny ribs and send him packing. I scare the shit out of him with wine and roses and stupid jokes he'll never in all eternity understand and I watch him tuck his tail between his legs and go cowering down the lane.

I am not moved by his furtive backward glances and the pitiful yelping of the Last Chance. All you have to do is pour yourself another glass, make yourself a salami sandwich with a clear conscience, and he goes scurrying into the bushes to sniff his old turds for comfort and consolation.

Read 'em and weep.

It's the oldest trick in the book, the wooden horse at the door after a lifelong siege. Did you forget that the village Ettore and I are approaching tonight was built over a city that was made with the spoils of Troy long before you changed your tune. We built our houses over it and I played in its ruins even before I learned to walk.

I was away and Don Ignazio came offering eggs, salamis, and salvation. How can you refuse, Ettore said, turning to nod again at the wrought iron cross behind us. "Go argue with trucks out of the sky and rich people bearing gifts," he said.

Back then, death and money shared the same bed. We hadn't learned to distinguish yet between the law that determined rainfall, landslides and earthquakes and the law that determines who got the eggs and salamis and who got the wild grasses and onions. It is only now, with my stomach full, that I am learning to refuse.

In the South, *no* was the unutterable. You could be swallowed in an earthquake for such gall. If you really had to, you just silently raised your eyes toward heaven.

How can you refuse, he repeated, with your father long dead, the other man in the family taking up with a whore in Canada, your mother getting old, hunger screaming at your door, and your husband God knows where.

A volunteer in Abyssinia — I found myself interjecting, even though I knew that being far away, honourably or not, was not the point — and then a prison camp in Scotland.

"Right. You volunteered for Africa. You were man enough to do what had to be done and there's not a person in town who doesn't respect you for it. A man has to make hard decisions and sometimes it's I'll shoot you if you go, knife you if you stay, forgive you if you throw yourself down the well, as the Ancient One said, and you did what a man has to do. Not like some of those piazza lumps who moaned about their flat feet or their gastro-intestinal this and that and their poor old mothers all alone and chirped about a new day dawning and how it takes a little while for a great empire to get on its feet, you know, and blamed the cowards and the traitors when Mussolini and the empire both got their balls yanked off. While you and men of respect like you were God knows where making something with your sweat and blood, sacrificing your lives for a little bread to send home to your families — where were they? Swatting flies in their doorsteps or shuffling around the post office waiting for some poor woman to get a letter from God knows where so they could give her the song and dance about their poor sick mamas and pinch her for half a lira. Or standing around good-morning-sir, good-evening-sir, with their hat in their hand licking the asses of Don This and Don That, hoping for a chance to run a message or scratch their balls for them, instead of taking the bull by the horns, biting the bullet, like you did and men of respect like you did, and doing what had to be done. You know what the Ancient One said: the pitying physician allows the wound to fester."

Ettore would have to continue like this for a while, speaking streams of apology and praise, not just to make sure I had not been offended, but to convince the powers above, who we weren't sure could decipher our language, that no complaint of any kind had been intended. Those who whine will have good reason, the Ancient One said.

Ettore and I both knew that hunger didn't allow for many lazy lumps in the piazza and that those who found themselves languishing in their doorsteps languished because it was their fate to languish. They were crippled or blind or heirs to the family estate. It was something else, perhaps unnameable, that Ettore was protesting about.

How can you refuse, he resumed; and the village was suddenly closer, not high over our heads any more, but in front of us, almost at eye level.

I think the sun was setting. It too would be almost at our level now, falling slowly into the sea behind us. And I hoped Ettore wouldn't stop talking as we drew close enough on the main road to make out the first dark specks of human figures against the golden sheen of winding streets.

" 'The whole village sings her praises and me, too,' Don Ignazio says to your cousin when they finally send him to make his intentions man-to-man and clear. 'I'm a man of honour,' he says, 'and I give my respect to those who deserve it. I'm no saint,' he says, 'and I don't think that leaving a basket of food at her door is going to give me a place in heaven, but her goodness, her kindness, her virtue and veneration, well it touched me,' he says with — and I swear this is true — his hand on his heart, 'and if I can do just this little thing for her, just this simple acknowledgement that goodness isn't always pissed on, then I can say that Don Ignazio Aritti is a man who doesn't close his eyes to justice.' He was touched all right, but God knows where. He started to spew so much nonsense to everybody about helping those who help others and being just and giving good its due that we all thought it was just a matter of time before he shaved his head and shut himself up in the monastery at San Bruno."

Ettore must have pondered his mission long and hard. By pausing now and then to study my face, gauging the anguish or bewilderment, the fear or shame, he anticipated my questions and was able to deal with them before my panic erupted. Still, the gold of the village darkened into amber and the growing specks drew longer shadows on the nearing streets and soon we would be able to make out the arms and legs and faces that would have a different story to tell.

"Who could tell? All of a sudden the miserly worm — God bless his soul — gets rid of the tax on hoes and axes and starts sharing fifty-fifty with his tenants. Hands out bottles of wine to his people on St. Martin's, oranges and small sacks of charcoal on the Epiphany. Then he stops swearing and telling dirty stories at the barbershop and goes to church every single day. He starts building a shrine to Our Lady of the Graces with his own hands near the top of Monte Cuccoli. Hauls bags of cement and mortar up on his back and spends the night up there when he's too exhausted to get down. So Maria accepts the gifts — it's not as if she were the only one."

We were coming to the last bridge, over the last river, the Torrente Felliri, where far below in the deafening whirlpool of spray and thunder some women were still beating laundry against the smooth boulders that broke the eddies of the river edge. Ettore, like everyone else who ever crossed the Felliri, stopped speaking as the first cool pinpricks of spray brushed our faces and we crossed the stone bridge in silence.

Near the end of the second bottle it is comforting to think of all those before us who had to defer to silence when they approached the Felliri. Those first to leave, the men from the village who had to stop their anxious chattering as they crossed the first bridge on their long way to Taranto, Aulis, and Troy.

To imagine what just and awesome geometry Pythagoras and his tatterdemalion band heard bellowing in the cool spray and roaring vortex as they paused to listen again on their way to the higher knowledge and the mystic number of murder in Crotone.

Or Alaric marching south to his final river, in this valley or the next, where out of respect for the man they changed the course of the stream to hide his bones forever from the Rome he had destroyed.

Even Garibaldi, fresh from conquering multifarious Sicily, gathering more dreamers of oneness behind him, like a Pied Piper, on his way north to red and single victory.

At the end of the second bottle I include Aesop and Swinburne, Alcibiades and Lear, Coeur de Lion and Patton, Barbarossa and Pyrrhus, Guiscard and Saladin, and all the other countless, restless dreamers of lust and potent numbers who fell silent to the roar of the Felliri and who, like Ettore and me, paused for a moment to listen to its message.

When the last pinprick faded and the thunder of the river began to lag behind us, Ettore resumed the story as though there had been no interruption at all, with the same detached flourishes and drawn out sentences, as though we had all the time in the world, as though the village were an eternity and not just half an hour away.

"He never finished the shrine," he continued above the receding roar. "And I don't think anybody's too anxious to finish it for him, now that he had to be buried outside the walls, without the ear — which some cat or dog must have dragged away — even though it wasn't just his family who wanted him inside the cemetery.

"And it wasn't just his family in the funeral procession," he went on with a shrug. "Of course these rich people go all out bringing in the actors with the ribbons of knights and nobles of the Crown in their lapels to pose as cousins and uncles from Naples and Palermo, the fancy band in smart uniforms from the city, and contracting mourners in abundance from their estates, a whole wailing battalion of them in their professional black, crying their hearts out and tearing at their faces, chanting nonsense and wailing litanies of praise, 'when they came to him for bread he gave them cheese', 'for the goodness in his heart he had to part', 'he talked to Jesus and Jesus talked back'. But that was expected. What you should know, what you have a right to know, is that they weren't the only ones. There were some who cried and chanted and weren't getting paid for it. Better you hear it from me first. Thousand Pieces and the Captain and Shitdragger and Gianbattista Achille, Soriano and Snakefeet, they were all there, Easter dressed and Good Friday somber, their wives wailing with the best of them, 'gone like the ear that heard so many troubles', and Fast-as-me and Vincenzini, too blowing into their handkerchiefs and wiping a tear from their eye.

"All the ones who got the baskets and the sweeter deals were there, as if he were going to continue his largesse from the next world, push up mushrooms and truffles from hell if he didn't rain down manna from heaven for them. But it didn't work. Don Ignazio wasn't in the ground a month before things got back to normal, sixty-forty, the tax on anything made of iron, just the way it always was, and an extra measure from each milling to pay for the hundred masses Don Ignazio deserved."

I don't know what he saw the next time he paused to look at me, but the closer we got to the foot of the village, the less sure he became of his reading. Or perhaps he knew before I did that I wouldn't be going much further. He sped up the list of mourners at the interment of Don Ignazio Aritti in unconsecrated soil, whether to provide me with a complete roll call of my mortal enemies or whether to postpone the recounting of Maria's interment in consecrated ground, I no longer wanted to know.

Last Published Poem

Poem

Here
at the poetry
factory
the typewriters
rattle all night

A thousand
well caught
regrets
are inspected hourly
for obscenity
      Sentimentality
      Self-indulgence
and other
imperfections of form

And because
it is a humanistic
establishment
the seconds

go to the poor

(1995)

Postscript

RUSSEL KORDAS
Exhibition of Paintings
Hellenic American Union, Athens
Jan. 11-12, 1977

KORDAS is one of the few artists confident enough to deal in human terms. To strive for a unity of consciousness, for the unity of the human form in a fragmented world, means confronting the Minotaur at the end of the mazes that separate art from life. It means dealing with the walls of paradox that make the human figure both larger and smaller than the world it is born in. To create figures that are as lucid and concrete as the Attic landscape in which they were born, and to infuse them with a human tenderness as graceful and subtle as only mortality possesses, requires a conceptual and technical mastery of the highest order.

Look closely at Kordas's canvasses. The simplicity is dynamic. It vibrates with the penetration of the human paradox and sounds a profound serenity. The serenity we feel in seeing the landscapes and figures is the mythopoeic experience of what is ultimately possible: the uncompromised embodiment of timelessness and mortality, spirit and matter.

Look at the three figures, who engulf and are engulfed by space. Look at the portrait of his father, who is defeated by time and is victorious over it. The landscapes too reach the same limits. The same maze must be crossed to reach the Greek village, for it too is both more and less than stone and plaster.

No school or fashion in painting will reach the limits of these tensions and make them vibrate in equilibrium. It is a solitary journey. In going his own way, Kordas has cut through the tension between spirit and stone: he brings what is around us in daily life to his canvasses, where, without surrendering its material reality, he infuses it with a spiritual one as well. With his unique mastery, Kordas draws the tensions between the monumental and the lyrical as tautly as possible before sounding that high clear note that echoes with serene humanity.

APPENDIX

Saint-Denys-Garneau: 30th Anniversary   (*)

I must disguise this. For all I know he was invented by those old Quebecois scholars dreaming of other days. But I want to think that the real reason why I know so little about him is because his photograph in a little old school book is foggy. I sometime entertain the idea that it was planned that way, considering the lengths that even he himself went to protect his anonymous readers. So I should keep the impression as vague as possible. And maybe it too can diffuse far enough to vanish.

But we must allow for some scanty details from a poorly calculated plan he must have worked on. We must allow some images to stand out in the arguments he conducted with his notebook. And for that iron cross that was nailed to his chest, and especially for how he grew and swallowed it into his body. Like a tree trunk over a nail, like his conversion swallowing the host.

Now we can erase ourselves into the fog, the sweet mist in which he saw the whole universe dance. But we must avoid learning how it clotted into a shroud and suffocated the poetry in his legs. We must stumble lightly into the young mist, over the memory of our private clouds, and stop where he only began: the dance, the joy of out footsteps tapping out the rhythm. The overturned canoe, his head lying face down in the river is merely bad poetry.

---

*This prose composition, published in *Waves,* vol. 3, no. 1 (1974), may shed some light on Saro's conception and development of his poem "Saint-Denys-Garneau, an Autobiography," which he published one year later in *Applegarth's Folly,* no. 2 (London, Ontario, 1975). The poem appears above on page 33.

And now we can see him and Catherine Tekakwitha sitting by a frozen stream, discussing their scars, laughing at their authors. We can detect a wisp of the old dream in their eyes though they both know that the world is each man's mist, and footsteps each man's author.

A cousin of his said that he used to call light by its name and that the light would answer.

I think I was sixteen. I used to read the newspapers and found enjoyment in distinguishing between concrete and nebulous details. I especially liked the Saturday magazine section. I was very impressed once by a quotation in bold type on the margin of a French-problem article. It said something about an organization being set up to take revenge on the country that killed Saint-Denys-Garneau.

He came to mind again when I was thinking of what to do for an essay on Canadian Literature. For the purpose of that essay I allowed that new organization to be the FLQ.

In a French school book some of his poems had words missing and footnotes explaining that they were illegible. I suspected they were blasphemous.

I admit that I sometimes wondered what newspapers and traffic signs did to this dance.

In a Ph.D. thesis a monk said that great despair followed after the collapse of the delicate world which the young poet had woven. The monk more or less blamed it on the exotic dance materials the poet had used. The monk then added that after the inevitable collapse, the mature poet turned more purely, more precisely towards God. The monk quoted *Le Devoir* which said that the drowned poet had written the best religious poem ever seen on this continent, perhaps even the best in modern times. I admit that I was reminded of the fact that in Charleville there is an official holiday on Rimbaud's birthday.

I ran across the same general phrases in three books: on October 24, 1943, Saint-Denys-Garneau was feeling quite restless … very restless … somewhat anxious.

It is almost as certain that he then paddled his canoe to an island he used to go to, that he began to feel somewhat anxious, that he went for help at a nearby house, and that his body was found beside a stream the next day.

His cousin said that he had offered himself to light and that the light accepted him.

Immigrant Songs (*)

1.

My father forgives me anything

The senseless universities
not making things better
after all, my vague Canadian
pain, even my Protestant friends
ashamed of the money

He has forgiven Canada
for his old age

He has forgotten the war-crazy
rich who kidnapped him from
his family for twelve years

He goes to Mass every day
and still prays
for those who are alone

While I, escaping to Greece
learned nothing: still struggling
to tell him I love you
through a useless English poem

---

*This is the first published version of this poem, which appeared in *Northern Journey* (1976). The second version, which Saro reworked to great effect, was anthologized in *Roman Candles* (1978) and appears above on page 47.

2.

Seared mangled summers
women in black, someone
always dying through
those endless families

"Calabria's Best Are Lost"
drifts through College Street
famines retold in songs, sons
in universities, the same

old moon: the South has always
bled this way, the music
runs empty through these once
fabled streets, the South

bleeds hollow, the old
blood coagulates, a maze
of tourniquets swelling
through a lively memory

Bloodflakes crystallize
on their Canadian daughters
on their hidden lipsticks
and dreams of fair Canadian
boys, of cars in the night

Congealing over their aching
and sacred southern cunts:
just one bursting seal, another
memory of southern love, like

clay bloodflakes on the boots
of construction workers
walking home

Sister, don't you see
your clotted blood gathers
on our fathers' boots, and
we're all just trying
to make it run free again
make it burn with the old
family fire, because

At our loud weddings
the eyes of our fathers
would bleed with joy
and ache with good wishes
anticipating that ecstatic
moment when the new husband
displays the First Night
sheets in triumph

Sister, let us set our mixed
blood on even wilder fire
and burn all those whose souls
and lands do not run red

3.

This young man that I know,
born in a village not far
from mine, laughs about how
he leans his chair back from
the desk, further and further
until he is about to fall
over, all this after having
placed his father's anvil
strategically behind him
so that he would break
his neck if he went too far.

When he tires of this, he
pins his back against one end
of the room and dashes for
the opposite wall with his head
firmly forward, always stopping,
as he puts it, within a hair's
breadth of an open skull.

I told him that at his age
I merely wished my family
and all Calabria dead a few
times before reaching for
the Valium and putting Cohen
loudly on the stereo.

4.

Poetry at best
leaves me cold

My father suffered more
indignities than I with
a degree in English could
ever dream of conjuring

After all, it's no way
to avenge his or any strangled life

He thinks I am unhappy
because I write
and this makes him only
more resigned, to think
that after all these countries
even his youngest son
has not escaped

I should leave this unreal
language and I should tear
down all the sub-divisions
he laid cement for:

He has not built my prison

I should raze all Calabria
and perhaps then say, Father

I am sorry for these songs
let us build a new life
somewhere else again

BIBLIOGRAPHY

Primary Sources

Poems

"Alex Colville's Horse." In *Impulse*, vol. 3, no. 2 (Toronto, 1974).

"Slow Death." In *Other Voices* (London, Ont., 1974).

"Someday." In *Waves*, vol. 2, no. 3 (1974).

"I used to." In *Waves*, vol. 2, no. 3 (1974).

"Saint-Denys-Garneau, an Autobiography." In *Applegarth's Folly*, no. 2 (London, Ont., 1975).

"Immigrant Songs." In *Northern Journey* (1976).

"Corfu Afternoon." In *The Antigonish Review* (1977).

"Gifts." In *The Antigonish Review* (1977).

"Travel." In *The Canadian Forum* (June-July 1978).

"Wake." In *Roman Candles*. Ed. Pier Giorgio Di Cicco. Toronto: Hounslow Press, 1978.

"Canadian Poet." In *Roman Candles*. Ed. Pier Giorgio Di Cicco. Toronto: Hounslow Press, 1978.

"I Ching in March." In *Roman Candles*. Ed. Pier Giorgio Di Cicco. Toronto: Hounslow Press, 1978.

"Immigrant Songs." In *Roman Candles*. Ed. Pier Giorgio Di Cicco. Toronto: Hounslow Press, 1978.

"Poem." In *Roman Candles*. Ed. Pier Giorgio Di Cicco. Toronto: Hounslow Press, 1978.

"Looking Back." In *Waves*, vol. 6, no. 3 (Spring, 1978).

"Seduction Poem 2 (Love and Death)." In *Waves* (1981).

"Poem." In *Quiebre*, no. 1 (Apr. 1995).

Fiction

"The Feast of St. Joseph." In *Gamut International* (Dec. 1987).
"Saint-Denys-Garneau: 30th Anniversary." In *Waves,* vol. 3, no. 1 (1974).

Secondary Sources

Amprimoz , Alexandre L., and Dennis F. Essar. *"La Poétique de la mort: La poésie italo-canadienne et italo-québécoise d'aujourd'hui." Studies in Canadian Literature / Études en littérature canadienne,* vol. 12, no. 2 (1987).

Boelhower, William. "Italo-Canadian Poetry and Ethnic Semiosis in the Postmodern Context." *Canadian Literature,* vol. 119 (1988): 171-78.

Loriggio, Francesco. "Review of *Roman Candles." Quaderni d'italianistica, Journal of the Canadian Society for Italian Studies,* vol. 1, no. 2 (1980).

Pivato, Joseph. *Contrast: Comparative Essays on Italian-Canadian Writing.* Toronto: Guernica, 1985.

Teti, Vito. *Il senso dei luoghi.* Rome: Donzelli Editore, 2004.

Acknowledgements

Acknowledgement is made to Luciano Iacobelli and John Calabro of the Quattro Books team for their perseverance in securing funds for this volume when public funding to publish Saro D'Agostino's writing was not forthcoming. I am indebted to Lis Jakobsen for her trust in me to bring Saro's writing to press, as well as to Rita Davies, Barry Olshen, Glen McGuire and Pier Giorgio Di Cicco, who, by sharing their correspondence, have made for a more compelling publication. I would also like to thank Saro's brother and sister, Salvatore D'Agostino and Caterina Martini, of Toronto, as well as his uncle Domenico D'Agostino, his aunt Maria Pasceri and Saro's old teacher, Prof. Domenico Carnovale, whom I met in San Nicola da Crissa, and Saro's cousin, Tino D'Agostino, of Vibo Valentia, for their hospitality and for sharing their knowledge of Saro and so many other things of value to this project. Among the many supporters who shared their memories of Saro, Sam Pupo and Karol Orzelski deserve special mention, as do Isabella Colalillo-Katz, Joseph Maviglia, Gianna Patriarca, John Romano, Ewald Schaeffer, Gonzalo Bernardos, Daniel Dahan and Graziano Marchese, all poets and friends from Dooney's, the usual suspects who took this project to heart from the beginning. I also wish to remember Martin Britstone, a friend of Saro's whose suicide preceded Saro's. I am grateful as ever for the privilege to count on the support and editorial expertise of Cy Strom, as well as on the friendship of Vito Teti, Ciccio Bellissimo, William Boelhower, Tina Scatozza and Wladimir Krysinski, over the years. Finally, I wish to commend the staff of the Thomas Fisher Rare Book Library, University of Toronto, and Bonnie McIsaac at *The Antigonish Review,* St. Francis Xavier University, for their bibliographical expertise and for all their help. This book is dedicated to Sarah Stewart, Saro D'Agostino's daughter. To Franceline and my son, Domenico (Mico), who also believe, goes all my love.

About the Author

Born July 11, 1948, in San Nicola da Crissa, Calabria, Rosario (Saro) D'Agostino came to Toronto with his mother, Rosa, in 1953. His father, Nicola, had preceded them in 1950. When in 1960 the father decided to go back to Italy, Saro returned to his place of birth with his parents. It was not until 1962 that they were all back together in Toronto.

In 1972 Saro graduated from York University's Glendon College with a degree in English Literature. He travelled to Europe in the summer of 1973 – Holland, Germany, France, Greece, Italy – and visited his village in Calabria that August, but only briefly. During this trip his Mediterranean sensibility was captivated by Greece, and that is where he would return for extended stays with friends and lovers numerous times between 1973 and 1980, with the project to be *free from the harness of a settled life in Toronto* and to write.

In the early 1970s he began to publish poetry in a number of respected Canadian magazines, among them *Impulse, Applegarth's Folly, The Antigonish Review, Waves, Northern Journey* and *The Canadian Forum*. He was a significant contributor to *Roman Candles*, a landmark anthology of poems by seventeen Italo-Canadian poets edited by Pier Giorgio Di Cicco (Toronto: Hounslow Press, 1978). A number of these poems were further anthologized in *Italian Canadian Voices*, edited by Caroline Morgan Di Giovanni (Oakville: Mosaic Press, 1984 and 2006), and in *L'Altra Storia*, a bilingual anthology of Italian-Canadian writing edited by Francesco Loriggio (Vibo Valentia, Italy: Monteleone Editore, 1998).

Through the 1970s, Saro had long and fulfilling love relationships with first Rita Davies and later Jocelyn Laurence. By the early 1980s, following the end of both relationships, he had married, and a daughter, Sarah, was born. Saro obtained his Ontario teacher's certification and for several years taught grade school in Toronto.

When this marriage ended in divorce and he was diagnosed as suffering from depression, he took an extended leave. Saro never returned to full-time employment, but sought to continue to write. By now he was frequently under the influence of prescribed medication and substance abuse.

Saro was married a second time, to Lis Jakobsen, in 1987.

At no time an aggressively enterprising promoter of his own writing, Saro never published a book when he was alive. On the insistence of friends Alfredo Romano, Mario Romano, Haygo Demir and Antonino Mazza he contributed a superb surreal prose piece, "The Feast of St. Joseph," to *Gamut International* (1987), which he described as an excerpt from a novel in progress. It was among the last works he published. Months before his suicide from a prescription drug overdose on September 22, 2000, he had already announced that he had erased his hard drive. Only "Maria," a novella, survived, which together with previously published and unpublished poems and fiction, and a selection of Saro's letters, is here published for the first time.

About the Editor

Antonino Mazza is the author of acclaimed translations of Eugenio Montale, *The Bones of Cuttlefish* (1983), and of Pier Paolo Pasolini, *Poetry* (1991). For the latter he was awarded the Italo Calvino Translation Prize by Columbia University (1992). He has published two books of his own poetry, one of which, *The Way I Remember It* (1992), was first released as a recording with his musician brother Aldo Mazza (1988), choreographed by the Vancouver-based E.D.A.M. Dance Company and widely performed. For the same book published in Italian translation, *La nostra casa è in un orecchio cosmico* (Monteleone Editore, 1998), he was the recipient of the 2001 Grotteria Prize. His reissue of Mario Duliani's *The City Without Women: A Chronicle of Internment Life in Canada During World War II* won the Brutium "Calabria" Gold Medal in Rome and inspired the NFB documentary *Barbed Wire and Mandolins* (1997). More recently he has published *Urban Harvest* (2004) and other creative non-fiction works and contributed English translations of younger Italian poets to *Italville, an Anthology of New Italian Writing*, published in Canada by Exile Editions (2006). In 2009 he was the recipient of the Savuto-Cleto Cultural Association Community Achievement Award. He lives in Ottawa and teaches at Carleton University.